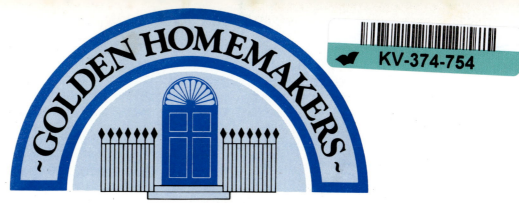

GOLDEN HOMEMAKERS

Secondhand bargains made new

Marshall Cavendish London & New York

Introduction

Renovating yesterday's furniture for use in a modern setting is something almost everyone would like to be able to do at one time or another. If brand new, modern furniture is not to your taste or real antiques are too costly, you can try refinishing an old table with a badly scratched surface or painting a set of dining chairs in gay colours or re-upholstering a tatty old sofa.

This Golden Homemaker volume gives you precise step-by-step directions on the how-to of all these projects as well as dozens of inspirational ideas to get you started. You can learn the secrets of bringing a dull-looking finish back to life or applying a completely new one – from stripping, bleaching and liming to staining, painting and polishing. Or re-cane a broken chair seat or re-upholster one using foam padding.

For those unusual items – china, glass, silver – which you may have collected over the years, there are instructions on cleaning and mending, as well as information about pewter, chrome, copper and brass.

Lovers of old clocks will also find valuable information on repairing and replacing parts. There are novel suggestions for bringing quaint but obsolete objects back into use – pretty lamps from coffee grinders, tables from old sewing machines. Whatever your tastes you can create a truly individual look with your furniture and turn those bargains into handsome additions to your home.

Contents

© Marshall Cavendish Limited 1973, 1976
Published by
Marshall Cavendish Publications Limited
58 Old Compton Street,
London W1V 5PA

ISBN 0 85685 181 7

Printed in Great Britain by
Petty and Sons Limited, Leeds.

SECOND-HAND BARGAINS MADE NEW

Finding unusual furniture for the home is fun — and especially rewarding if you come across a bargain. Often the most original or inspiring interiors are those which have been carefully put together from a range of assorted furniture styles and finishes — richly grained polished woods and veneers of almost any period, painted or stained chairs and tables of a more modern, mass-produced variety, or huge, old cupboards and chests brought to life with linings of pretty paper.

Variety of finishes

Whatever your tastes, most second-hand furniture can be refinished to suit you. Whether you want to strip wood to enhance the grain, give it a shiny polish, stain it a brilliant colour, paint it with a gloss finish or decorate it with unusual designs, it's quite easy to do if you follow a few basic rules when you first examine your chosen piece. You can even give wood a ready-made antique finish using a proprietary preparation.

What to avoid

Never attempt to renovate anything which might be valuable or classed as an antique — if in doubt consult an expert before doing any work.

Look at all structural repairs, such as broken chair or table legs, damaged upholstery or badly chipped wood, in relation to your own practical skills. Simple repairs for beginners are given in this book, but if you have to pay a skilled craftsman to repair a piece for you, you will no longer have a bargain.

Finally, examine all wood for traces of woodworm — it's death to furniture and can easily infect any wooden structures. It can be identified by fine round holes and powdery wood dust. Very mild cases can be treated with proprietary anti-woodworm solutions, but advanced cases are difficult to cure, so avoid them.

Other 'junk' items

Apart from wooden furniture, other useful or decorative bits and pieces will benefit from some renovation. Silver, glass, china — and things made from copper, brass, chrome or marble — can be given new life with a bit of careful work, so don't pass them by.

Remember: with careful examination and preparation, you can make a secondhand bargain into an attractive addition to any home.

WHAT TO LOOK FOR

Most of the old furniture you will come across will be made almost entirely of wood, which was available to craftsmen of earlier times in copious quantities and great variety. To make the best possible assessment of secondhand pieces, the more you know about wood the better.

Grain markings

In temperate conditions trees make new tissue at a very high rate in the spring, but slower in the summer, and concentric rings of wood are added as it grows fatter. Spring growth is lighter coloured and somewhat softer than the narrower bands of summer wood — which form 'annual rings', most marked in softwoods.

How logs are cut up

It is the tree's annual rings of summer tissue that form the characteristic grain stripes of the wood when the trunk is sawn lengthwise into boards and battens.

By no means all the log is usable wood, so the timber merchant's main concern is to get as much saleable material as he can. He normally slices softwoods into slabs, with parallel sawcuts which give him a good chance of wasting little but the bark and the central pith of a sound log. Although this method yields perfectly adequate timber for common building purposes, it is far from satisfactory for furniture. Every plank, except those on either side of the pith, tends to curl up away from the centre as it dries out and ages. The middle two planks have equal stresses on both broad surfaces so their movement is minimal.

Quarter-sawn virtues

Looking at these centre-slice boards end-on, you will see that the ring markings are almost at right angles to their faces. This feature is what you should look for to check whether your wood is radially sawn. Some boards will be cut perfectly 'on the quarter' ('quarter sawn' and 'radially sawn' are often used interchangeably). This method means that only four pieces can be removed from a log, so various patterns of log conversion have been evolved to give customers fairly stable stock at reasonable prices. Quarter sawing is inevitably more expensive than plain sawing because it wastes a good part of the log.

Grain figure

Some hardwoods are sawn radially for another reason. They have very visible rays — thin curtains of storage cells which are hung in straight lines radiating from the centre of the tree to its perimeter. Softwoods have them as well but they are not visible and the hardwood ones only show themselves to full advantage in fully quarter-sawn planks. For this reason you may see timber in some merchants' catalogues that is advertised as 'quarter sawn but not necessarily fully figured'. Not that there aren't other kinds of grain figure, resulting perhaps, from twisting growth or knots but rays in hardwoods are the main source where solid wood is concerned.

Veneers

Exotic, richly hued and beautifully figured timbers have always been in shorter supply than run-of-the-mill varieties. As well as being scarcer, the knotted or twisted kinds are by and large too weak structurally to be of much use in normal joinery. Knowing this, many successive generations of carpenters have used such wood in thin sheets to veneer plainer but stronger materials. Rarer veneers became expensive, and naturally fell into the hands of only the most skilful craftsmen. They developed the art of matching veneers: taking adjacent sheets from the same log, which of course had the same figuring, and arranging them in symmetrical patterns to cover broad surfaces.

Know your timbers

As species and sub-species run literally into the thousands, you would need to be an expert indeed to name different woods on sight. However, in the secondhand furniture field, you have a relatively small selection to familiarize yourself with. If starting from scratch, buy a set of educational samples from a merchant and study the grains, which are a surer guide than colour (often disguised by varnish). Look at a lot of museum pieces. This will give you a fair idea of which kinds of wood are used to make different sorts of pieces. Always try to see through the finish to the wood, so that you don't scrape off or paint over anything worth salvaging.

Know your finishes

There are few surface finishes on furniture which are incapable of being restored, so don't bypass a charming piece just because its surface is in bad condition.

Some finishes cover up the wood underneath or disguise it, while others enhance the wood without covering the grain. Below is a quick guide to the basic types of finishes and where you might expect to find them:

Oiled finishes will darken the wood but allow the grain and texture to show through. Oak, deal and beech furniture was traditionally finished with oil and wax, or with oil and a turpentine-gum based varnish. The latter is not used today.

Wax polishes were traditionally made from a mixture of beeswax, turpentine and carnauba wax. Modern wax finishes are made with silicone ingredients and are more resistant to marking. This type of polish is used mainly to protect another finish, such as oil.

Varnishes come in numerous varieties and combinations. Some are based on natural wood resins, others on synthetic cellulose constituents, and still others are based on shellac and a volatile spirit mixture.

Older types of furniture were often covered with varnishes known as lacquers, which were usually spirit varnishes. Most mass-produced furniture made within the last 40 years (except reproduction furniture and that with a polyurethane finish) was covered with a cellulose-based lacquer. This can be identified by the thick, layered appearance of the surface coating.

French polish is a traditional finish often found on antique furniture. It is composed chiefly of shellac dissolved in methylated spirits, but the mirror-like surface which is characteristic of this polish is achieved through the actual polishing technique.

Painted finishes are, of course, easily recognized. If you find a fairly old painted piece, do not be too hasty about removing the paint. Some old paints can in themselves make a piece of furniture valuable. If in doubt, seek a professional appraisal.

Caveat emptor
(Let the buyer beware)

Never mind the dirt or the broken legs, but avoid loose joints in any quantity, panels with broad cracks in them or tide-marked wood betraying exposure to damp. Above all, keep a sharp lookout for signs of attack by fungi and wood-boring pests. Train your nose to differentiate between the dusty and the musty. Shun pieces with clumsy repairs that destroy the original character of the piece: screws visibly placed, nailed patches, metal rods or wires. Most broken legs can be repaired, the simpler ones possibly replaced. But if you come across an elaborately curved one with a compound fracture involving splits down the grain and loss of timber, remember that you won't be able to mend or to replace it yourself unless you have skills equivalent to those of the original maker.

The table: You may find a deep dovetail joint (inset left) where apron and side join the leg top. If you do not want to replace the joint with hand-made dovetails, use dowels.

The top is usually held down by turn buttons (inset right). These are not glued, since they have to be free to slide a little in their grooves as the top wood shrinks with time.

The chest with sagging drawers: There are often small plywood anti-wear pads, pinned and glued to the drawer rails. If you replace them, lay the new pieces with the top grain running from back to front, otherwise the sliding action of the drawer may splinter them. Use a diamond with a point facing front (inset right).

The drawer-separating rails are probably fitted into the sides with stub tenons (inset left) so are not easily replaced. You must cut out worn corners and fit matching inserts.

The chest's top is fixed on to struts joined to the frame with small dovetails.

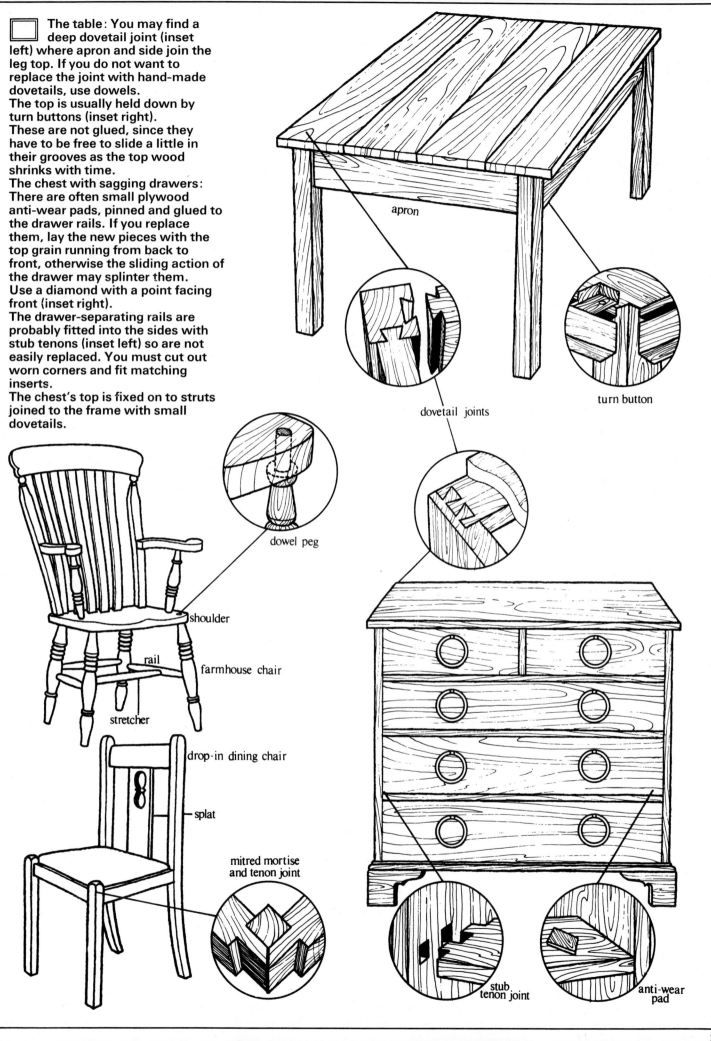

apron

turn button

dovetail joints

dowel peg

shoulder

rail

farmhouse chair

stretcher

drop-in dining chair

splat

mitred mortise and tenon joint

stub tenon joint

anti-wear pad

BASIC CLEANING AND RENOVATING

In the cold light of home, you will probably be able to make a more detailed and objective assessment of the state of your find than was possible when you first examined it. Remember, if it looks a fine, well-made piece of furniture, have it appraised by an expert before you do any work on it — some pieces are worth more in their original (possibly damaged) state than they would be after any but expert restoration.

Identifying the polish
Patina, the deep surface finish that is built up by the years and loving care, cannot be instantly recreated, so never remove it unless it is absolutely unavoidable. Be especially careful with oiled and waxed finishes on stained or natural wood. Applied finishes such as varnish, French polish or paint can be touched up in local spots if necessary. However modern finishes differ considerably in composition from old ones and it may be difficult, without experience, to achieve a good match with materials that will adhere to and blend in with the old surface. A bit of careful experimentation on scraps of wood or unseen areas of the furniture can prove invaluable.

To distinguish one finish from another rub real turpentine (not a mineral substitute) onto a small area with a soft cloth, where the spot will not show. If the wood has been oiled and waxed, a rub or two with the turpentine will take you down to the bare wood. If a polished surface is still visible after the turps test, rub on a little methylated spirit. The surface will go sticky and soft if it has been French polished.

Yet another test for ascertaining a finish is to scrape a small, unnoticeable area with a razor blade. French polish should produce very thin shavings or curls; oil varnishes produce thicker shavings; and cellulose varnishes will only scrape to powder.

If you decide to refinish completely, you will of course have to start by stripping off the old top-dressing. This is a major operation, dealt with more fully on pages 10 and 11. But what about simple cleaning and retouching?

Beware of the bathtub
Whatever you do, don't pour gallons of soapy water over it and scrub it clean. Dirt may respond to this treatment, but the wood may not like it at all. Two major problems are likely to occur from such treatment: the wood will either become flexible and warp, or its moisture content will rise above 20 per cent so that it begins to rot. Either way, the dampness will make the grain rise, because spring wood absorbs water more quickly than summer growth. This is how the ridges occur on scrubbed deal table tops. Hardwoods react far less violently, certain types having tremendous natural resistance to penetration. Chestnut, oak and teak are the ones you are likely to come across, but pieces made from these should still not be scrubbed or doused, for fear of water affecting the animal glue which holds the joints together.

Solvents and scrape
If your piece is relatively lightly soiled, a well-squeezed washleather and mild detergent may be enough to clean it. Nothing more astringent should be tried on French polish, but paints, varnishes or lacquers could be cleaned with any proprietary paint cleaner. After washing and thoroughly drying the wood you can decide whether the surface needs nothing more than a good waxing, or whether any scratches, dents or burns need repairing or retouching before the piece can be used. (See pages 8, 9, 10, 11.)

Removing old wax
Before any repair can be made which involves applying fresh French polish all trace of wax polish and sticky oil must be removed. Where you intend confining your repairs to a local patching job, subsequently merging new polish into the old, use cotton wool soaked in a mineral turpentine substitute to mop the surface and dissolve the wax, followed by a good scrub with a clean, absorbent rag. Knitting needles or suitably whittled hardwood sticks are useful for getting into the moulding crannies.

As it is now so easy to apply a proprietary French polish on top of the old, you may decide to repolish the piece completely. If so, you could use very fine steel wool instead of cotton wool to clean the surface. Small areas of damaged French polish can be removed in the same manner using a proprietary varnish remover, or very strong ammonia.

Paints and varnishes
You can treat small areas of paint, varnish or lacquer in a similar way, with an appropriate solvent.

Test for the best solvent to use on a small, unnoticeable area; methylated spirit, acetone, cellulose thinners or proprietary strippers are some common solvents. Always exercise extreme caution when working with them; keep away from fire and be sure to work where there is good ventilation.

Remove the damaged area only, unless the whole surface has crazed into tiny cracks, or has badly bloomed to a milk-white opacity.

Veneers versus solids
Many pieces of old or secondhand furniture are entirely surfaced with sheets of polished veneer. A careful look at the end grain along the vertical edge of a flat surface will usually reveal enough of a difference in the grains for you to determine whether or not the piece is veneered. Repairs to veneered surfaces are discussed on pages 8, 9, but it is possible to deal with superficial scratches or marks as you would with solid wood.

It is essential to remember that a veneer is very thin and has been fixed on its base with Scotch glue, so great care must be taken not to let water or other solvents soak into the bare wood. If the water gets under the veneer, it will lift and you will have a very major restoration job to do. Veneers or marquetry inlays were never varnished with anything containing turpentine or its substitutes, as these would also have softened the glue. Quick drying volatile spirit varnishes were used instead.

Further considerations
Always think of the wood which lies beneath the surface finish and then decide what type of finish would best suit the appearance of the wood and the use to which you are going to put the piece. *Oiled finishes* darken wood without covering the grain or texture. The finish is quite tough, water resistant, and non-gloss. In general, softwoods are not suitable for oiling. *Wax polishes* are excellent protectors for oiled or French-polished surfaces. If applied to raw wood, the wood should first be sealed with a modern polyurethane sealer.

Varnishes will give wood a transparent, hard-gloss finish. As has been mentioned, there are many different types of varnish which have been used at different times on furniture. Modern synthetic surface finishes, composed of polyurethanes, give the same effect as varnishes. These are easy to apply and are more resistant to heat, water, scratches or spirits than either cellulose lacquers or French polish (the latter, especially, is very easily marked by liquids or heat).

If you do discover that your piece needs some structural repairs, tackle these before you touch up the finish — a variety of common repairs are described on pages 8 and 9.

Left: Many pieces of furniture only need a good clean and polish before they are fit for use. A dirty, greasy surface can generally be cleaned with a soft cloth and a solution of warm water and mild detergent – a pure white soap is very good.

Always wring out the cloth so that it is damp, not wet. Light wood, such as was used for the Welsh dresser, is often covered with sticky polish or even varnish or lacquer. Once you have removed the finish, you may find the natural grain only needs a good wax for protection.

Below: When cleaning a wood surface, be sure you do not take off the deep mellow patina by using very abrasive tools. Old wax can be removed by a very light rub with scouring powder and a dry cloth (never use water), and an appropriate grade of steel wool is best for crevices and turnings.

TOOLS AND HOW TO USE THEM

When renovating secondhand furniture the correct use of a few basic tools will make all the difference between a haphazard and a professional-looking job.

Personal protection equipment

An enormous amount of the work involved in renovating things consists of hard, dirty tasks, involving exposure to dust, chemicals and assorted nuisances of various kinds. Think ahead and protect yourself adequately. It is really only common sense to use breathing masks, safety goggles, barrier creams or gloves. Suit them to the job: for example, use plastic gloves instead of rubber ones when you have oils, greases or petroleum-derived solvents to deal with. Any of these will quickly make rubber gloves swell to twice their original size and finally disintegrate.

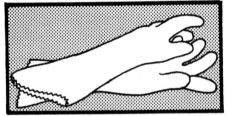

Cabinet and makeshift scrapers

To a carpenter, a scraper means considerably more than a sharp edge dragged at right angles across a wood surface. What he uses is a razor-keen, smoothly honed steel blade with the cutting edge burred over at a fairly acute angle to form a minute hook which slices off incredibly fine shavings from the timber. The finish which is left on the wood is so smooth that only a rub with the finest abrasive paper is needed to finish off. Today, it would probably be a very experienced craftsman who had mastered the techniques of sharpening and using the traditional hand scraper, and he would almost certainly have made it himself from a piece of silver (saw) steel.

Hand blades are still made by smaller tool firms, but the market leaders have concentrated on a two-handled model looking rather like an outsize metal spokeshave — far easier to sharpen and to use. Bevelled at 45°, its blade is honed exactly like a chisel, then the edge is turned over. Burnishers being scarce, smooth screwdriver blades are used instead. The set on this kind of scraper is produced by a small screw, mounted in the centre, which bends the edge downwards when it is turned.

Blades for these handled models have one curved edge for stripping off old paints and polishes quickly and one straight edge for finishing work. Their main drawback is that they are only meant to be used on flat or convex surfaces.

When you need a scraper to get into an angle or a rebate, the best solution is to turn over the edge of a chisel. Do not expect long life from a chisel converted to such a use and do not expect to use it for cabinet work ever again. All the same, you still need to use a good, plastic-handled type, to resist the pull of the scraping action.

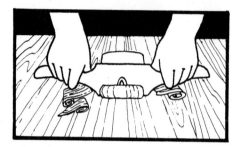

Holding devices

For some reason not easily explained, tools and equipment in this category seem to be the last that many people consider buying, whereas they are nearly the most important of all. No matter how many tools you may have, you will always have difficulty in working effectively unless you can hold things down firmly.

This does not necessarily mean that you must have a work bench, although there are some very compact, folding kinds now available. Portable vices mounted on trestles or tables, or even on stepladders, are a great help. (Always prop stepladders firmly open first.) Some self-grip wrenches have special clamps available as accessories, which enable them to be used as miniature vices. Multi-purpose vices offer tremendous versatility and value for money. They are probably the best type to get if you have no storage space and must manage all your repairs on the kitchen table.

Weights are another useful device to have. They make effective stabilizing influences on horizontal boards and can help a lot with gluing jobs — the only possible difficulty being that you must leave them in position until the setting is completely finished.

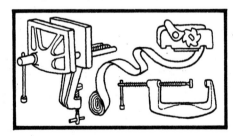

Reference tools

Straightedges are quite expensive, and easily worn untrue by constant duty as knife guides. Secondhand steel rules in the region of a metre long are reasonably priced and perfectly adequate for most of the jobs you are likely to do. If you intend using their graduations, look very closely before you buy them, to satisfy yourself that they are normal ones: some are made for pattern makers and carry 'stretched' measurement units to allow for contraction of the various metals upon removal from the casting mould.

Most try-squares are not as square on the outer edges as they are on the inner ones. Plastic stocks are usually accurate on both because the edges of the stocks can be machined parallel.

Spirit levels, like all reference tools, are only useful insofar as they remain accurate. To test a spirit level, place it on a known level surface. Take the reading and then turn the level around to see that it gives the same reading.

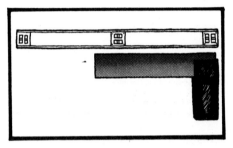

Marking and measuring

Steel tape rules provide the most helpful service. A good one will have a hook-end that slides to compensate for the tab thickness. If it did not, you would be that much out whenever you measured anything like a cupboard width for a shelf. It will also state the width of its case so that you can add this into a measurement if necessary.

Always mark wood with a knife or a gauge rather than a pencil. Knife lines are more precise, and the wood does not splinter across them. Scalpel or drawing knives are especially good for marking out, used with their low angle blades. If you want to do repairs involving mortice and tenon joints, get a combined gauge for parallel lines that will serve as an ordinary marking gauge as well.

Sawing

Hand-set saws are always easier to use. A junior hacksaw or a tenon saw should cope with most repairs, but before you buy a tenon saw, decide what kind of mitre box or sawing jig you want, if any. Some need larger saws than others.

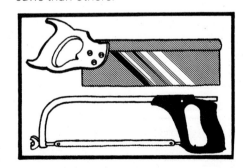

Shaping and smoothing

To cut down hardened resin filler quickly, one of the milled files sold with special holders is invaluable, particularly if you need to cut the filler down in or near a corner. Triangular or rat's tail files are also essential — some rather clever ones, such as Abrafile, are now available. These files have soft cores, so you can bend them to any odd shape you need for inaccessible places.

File handles are normally sold separately from their working ends. When you choose your own handles, look for solid plastic ones, or the wooden safety type which have a metal coil incorporated to prevent the metal end of the file piercing the wood.

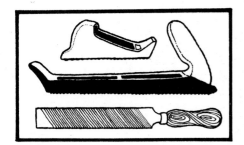

Chiselling

Although a chisel is probably the most efficient cutting tool in existence, it is also the most dangerous. Paradoxically, it is most potentially harmful when in least efficient condition, that is to say, when it is blunt.

The essential character of its edge is to be sharp, rigid and hard. Whatever force you put behind a chisel is distributed over this narrow cutting edge only. It should be kept razor-keen so that you never have to force it to do its work. Even when you hit the chisel with a mallet, to cut out a mortice for example, heavy blows should be totally unnecessary.

When properly sharpened, a chisel edge is bevelled only on the front; its back is kept absolutely flat to the oilstone to rub off the honing burr. This feature gives it the invaluable ability to cut exactly in line with its back. When working with a chisel always keep your eye on the back and not the axis of the handle. The two ought to be one and the same, but in practice they very rarely are.

Since you cannot keep your eye on two things at once, and you *must* keep it on the back alignment of the blade, only tap a chisel handle with the broad striking face of a mallet. If you use a hammer, you are very apt to slip and smash a finger or two.

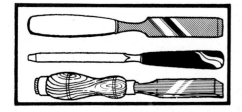

Drilling holes

Ordinary 'jobber's' drill twist bits are really designed for metal, but they will drill almost anything, except masonry. Being made to tight tolerances, they are good for making dowel-holes, especially in conjunction with a dowel jig. When drilling wood with them it is advisable to withdraw and clean any dust and bits out of the flutes every now and then. How far they will penetrate without sticking depends on the kind of wood.

There are special twist drills for wood which reduce in diameter towards the back more markedly than standard ones, but they are a little harder to find.

Ordinary auger bits may be up to a third of a millimetre ($\frac{1}{64}$-inch) in diameter bigger than the nominal size. For dowelling you will need the more accurate and therefore more expensive dowel bits, which tend to be a little short for use with dowel jigs.

Forstner bits need a steady hand, but produce usefully flat-bottomed holes. Guided by their cutting rim instead of by their point, they also come in handy for boring holes very near the edge of the wood. In this work it is easier to keep them straight if you have a ratchet brace.

Power drills need power-type bits, without screwed points and with extra-efficient chip clearance.

Masonry drills have tungsten carbide tips. This hard metal is made in several grades, but the tip hardness is not as important as the quality of the brazing between tip and drill body. Some will melt if you drill at over 1,000 rpm, while others will stand 3,000 with no protest. Bear in mind that single-speed drills normally turn at around 3,000 rpm.

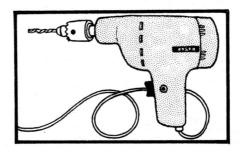

Screw driving

Wood screws are infinitely easier to use with screw-sink type pilot-hole bits, which make thread, shank and countersink-bevel preparation in one drilling. However, to get their full advantage you need a power drill. There is a different bit for each size and gauge of screw.

If you have to screw into chipboard, you will need to use special screws, such as the self-tapping ones. Ordinary ones do not get much of a grip in chipboard.

Ugly rust stains may appear in oak if you leave steel screws in it. This is because oak contains tannin which attacks the steel. Bright zinc-plated screws are better.

Planing

When planing surfaces on second-hand furniture, you may find that unseen nails or screws can chip the cutter edge of the plane, requiring it to be reground. The best general-purpose plane for unforeseen planing is one which has replaceable blades, such as the PTFE-coated planemaster type, with cheaply replaceable blades. These can rough down, smooth or rebate.

A small block plane for fine-finishing is also useful, preferably a $9\frac{1}{2}$, which has a mouth that can be closed up for work on curly grain.

Quick guide to adhesives

Animal glues are the traditional glues used by furniture makers. They are strong, quite flexible, but will not resist damp or heat. Scotch glue is an example.

PVA adhesives have generally superseded animal glues as the main adhesive for woodworking. They set in 20 minutes and dry in 24 hours.

Ureas are useful adhesives to use if you need to fill a gap and fix two things together (as with loose furniture joints).

Epoxy resins are the strongest and most versatile of the general-purpose glues. They are very good for mending glass and china as they are not affected by hot water.

Clear household adhesives are useful for most small, general repairs, but they are not especially strong. Do not use them on things subject to heat or hot water.

Natural latex is a tough, flexible adhesive designed for textile repairs. It will withstand washing in hot water, but not dry cleaning.

Rubber resin and synthetic latex adhesives will stick PVC tiles, rubber, and felt to concrete or hardboard. They will also join fabric, leather, ceramic tiles and reinforced plastic.

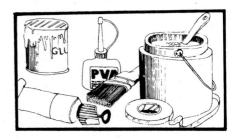

SIMPLE REPAIRS

Door and drawer locks (Fig. 1)

Having replaced worn, eroded or broken wood on the edge of a locking drawer or door, the lock-mortise chisel shown would be the best tool for re-cutting the mortise slot. This chisel is worked by striking it with a hammer, so it is possible to see exactly what you are doing. Cut the mortise by the 'crumbling' method shown. If you need to sink a plate, cut the housing out last.

Hinges (Fig. 2)

If the only fitting problem is filling in worn screw-holes, use small hardwood plugs chipped off with a chisel from a small, cross-cut piece of wood. Jam them in firmly behind the screws and sand down any protruding edges with abrasive paper.

When fitting hinges from scratch, mark all hinge positions by measuring from the same point, allowing for clearances (see right). A hinge's effective width is read at its thickest part, normally the pin, but look out for unusual types.

Broken legs and feet (Fig. 3)

Old breaks in ornamental legs or feet can rarely be repaired without some remaking. Fresh breaks in legs of any shape can be glued almost invisibly, but a connecting dowel is necessary for adequate strength.

To find the correct position for the dowel, tap a panel pin into one section of the break and file the end sharp. Press this end into the other section so that it marks where the dowel should go. Remove the pin and hand-drill a small hole in each part of the break. Use a drill bit the same diameter as the dowel, so that it will fit snugly into place. Chamfer the ends of the dowel and make a narrow groove along its length to allow excess glue to escape.

Broken or loose chair stretchers or rails (Fig. 4)

If you can match the timber, it is less trouble and takes less skill to replace a stretcher than to repair it. If you taper the tenons on the stretcher, you must 'spring' the leg joints as you slot in the tenons.

Broken or loose chair splats (Fig. 5)

It is usually possible to locate the top of the splat by looking for short dowels, or sometimes, sawn-off screws. When repairing, lever the bottom end into place before fixing it with dowels or screws which should be put in upwards through the lower rail of the chair back. This avoids visible repair scars and (provided the meeting surfaces are clean and well-glued) makes a firm fixing.

Burns or dents in solid tops (Fig. 6)

Ideally, you should remove a shallow burn mark by planing or sanding down the entire surface to the bottom level of the scraped-out depression. On a hardwood top, however, this would be too laborious and it is best to treat the hole only.

Most cigarette burns can be rubbed out of wood with a fine abrasive paper. A shallow burn can be coloured in with matching artist's oil paints and repolished when dry. Deep burns can be filled with coloured beeswax or epoxy resin. Fill burn holes in a French polished surface with a little semi-set polish. When dry, blend in the surface coat patch on top.

Dents in solid surfaces can usually be raised with a warm iron and a damp rag.

Local treatment for blemishes

These treatments are only for minor or superficial blemishes.

Scratches can be remedied with pro-

prietary scratch removers or rubbed out with flour paper which has been dipped in linseed oil. Fill deep scratches with melted beeswax, coloured slightly darker than the surrounding surface. When it has nearly set, rub it into the crack, and repolish the surface as appropriate.

Heat marks appear as white patches on cellulose and lacquer finishes and on French polish.

Rub with a 1 to 1 mixture of real turpentine and linseed oil, or real turpentine and camphorated oil. Clean off with vinegar and repeat the process until the mark has gone. You may also use a proprietary ring remover.

Alcohol is a solvent which will soften most polishes, so wipe up spills immediately, and leave the surface to set. If the alcohol has removed the polish, rebuild the area with coloured French polish applied with a small brush. Then rub it first with flour paper which has been dipped in linseed oil, and next with a soft pad until it blends in with surrounding areas. Superficial spirit or heat marks on semi-matt finishes can be removed with fine steel wool, but to obtain an even surface, you may need to rub over the entire surface. Then rewax with furniture polish.

Black marks are usually caused by water which has seaped beneath the finish. To repair them, the finish must be removed. Oxalic acid crystals are then added to a cup of water until no more will dissolve (a saturated solution), and the mark is swabbed with this. Oxalic acid does not damage finishes, so it will safely remove superficial ink stains as well.

Dents, burns or bubbles on veneered tops (Fig. 7)

Dents that penetrate a veneer surface need a carefully matched patch set in – not an easy job. If, however, the dent is superficial, you can sand through the top surface until the criss-cross marks made by toothing planes on the base can *just* be seen. Then stop and refinish.

Bubbles in veneers are caused by glue failure. Find and cure the cause (damp, fungus, bleach) then nick the bubble along the grain with a pointed knife. Work more hot-melt Scotch glue under the surface with the same knife and press down carefully with a warm iron and a damp rag.

Sticking or sagging drawers (Fig. 8)

Sticking is usually caused by swollen wood – a product of damp. If this is the case, use chalk to establish exactly where the trouble is, then plane, shave or sand away the excess wood. Seal with oil or lacquer to stop more moisture from entering the drawer and drawer rail.

Gate leg tables: rule joints (Fig. 9)

The only reason for a good quality gate leg joint to stick or bind is failure of the finish to keep out moisture, which then swells the wood just enough to give trouble. Often, all you need do to cure it is to put the piece in a dry atmosphere for a few days. If this does not work, the hinge will have to be moved over about 2 mm ($\frac{1}{16}$ inch) to allow the flap free movement.

Panels split at the joins (Fig. 10)

Panels are not normally glued into their supporting grooves, but are left free to slide, so that the furniture will not warp under the strain of the wood shrinking with age. It is often possible to reglue joints between panel components, using temporary screws or pins at the back to wire or string them together until the glue sets. Use hot-melt, animal glue, compatible with the original glue.

Panels split in the grain (Fig. 11)

Since no great strength is demanded of panels, the pieces used for them are often short-grained in places. With age, they warp and can rarely be reglued. Narrow cracks can be disguised with appropriately coloured wood stopper (slightly darker than the raw wood). If the cracks are wide and you do not want to paint the wood, it may be necessary to replace the whole panel, but this is not an easy job.

Beading and moulding repairs (Fig. 12)

If you can match the old beading closely enough to be unnoticeable, it is preferable to replace complete sections rather than small portions. Often it is not possible to get a good match, in which case the damaged piece should be cut out so that the new wood can be 'keyed' in. Match the shape of the new wood to the original by using very narrow planes. Web clamps are helpful to secure the new piece when gluing it in place.

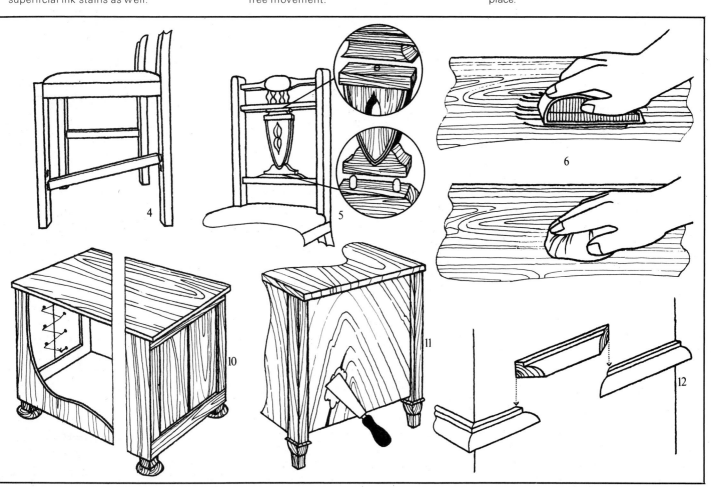

If you have decided that it is necessary to remove the old finish completely from a piece of furniture, you will find that you are faced with a choice of methods. Make it logically.

Look before you leap is a very sound adage in any context, but especially so where the shifting of old finishes is concerned. Difficult though it may be to guess what could be underneath an opaque coating, you should at the very least establish whether it is solid wood or veneer. (See page 2.) And by all means decide whether or not the piece can tolerate a complete stripping job — some solvents can be very hard on joints or on the wood itself. If you suspect that the piece, or perhaps just the finish alone, may be valuable, do not take any action without first taking expert advice.

Stripping methods

Chemical strippers are by far the easiest and most effective to use on furniture. Milder solutions will remove French polish (methylated spirit) or cellulose lacquers (ammonia), but it may make for peace of mind to use a proprietary chemical stripper suitable for the particular finish you want to remove. This way you shed all the will-it-won't-it worry and get clear and reliable instructions on what you need to do to remove residues. N.B. Strippers are strong chemicals, so take the obvious precaution against fumes, drips and skin contact. Should chemicals get on to your skin or in your eyes, rinse immediately with cold water.

Hard scraping to remove a finish will damage the wood but you should not have to do any, as the proper stripper will lift and soften the film for you. Thick or otherwise obstinate coverings sometimes need extra time for the chemicals to soak in or even additional applications of the stripper before any scraping is begun. Whenever the instructions offer a choice, wash the stripped wood with methylated spirit or a mineral turpentine substitute rather than water.

N.B. Some solvents will darken the wood, so again, it is always wise to do a patch test first. If you do not want the wood darkened, you will need to bleach it after stripping.

To bleach or not to bleach?

The main reasons for bleaching wood are to lighten the overall colour or to remove local staining, but you may

not need to bleach at all. A certain degree of natural variation in colour density, or shade differences between boards, can add to the honesty of appearance and give character to an ordinary piece of furniture.

What to bleach with
Ordinary domestic bleach is very dilute, far too mild for drastic work on wood. Stronger mixes of it can be made with crystals, but be careful to add crystals to water, NOT water to crystals. The reason for this lies in the heat which may be generated on contact; a small quantity of water could quickly boil and spit. Try to obtain pre-mixed bleach solutions whenever possible.

Sodium hypochlorite is very good for removing colour from wood, but if you have ink or iron stains to deal with, oxalic acid is better: about 100 grammes to a litre of water, if you buy it in crystal form. Always remember that, like most other bleaches, it is a first-class poison and a skin-stripper.

Two-part bleaches are the most powerful of all. They are very likely to attack the Scotch glue used for most joints and can lift veneers. Beware of using them.

Filling holes and cracks
Repairing a surface for opaque paints or lacquers is no trouble at all because you can use a variety of stopping compounds, not bothering about their colours. It is when you come to patch up blemishes for the finer, translucent varnishes, or for French polish, that complications set in.

Few, if any, fillers absorb stain or lacquer as readily as natural wood, so there is usually a need for some experimentation to secure a good blend of colour. The alternative techniques are to stain the stopping before you put it in or to use a ready-coloured kind, a bit darker than the surrounding wood.

Bruises in wood surfaces can be levelled up with a warm iron and a damp rag. Small scratches, dents or burns may not need a stopper covering if you are finishing with French polish. First, gently scrape out the damaged places to get a good key. Then allow the air to get to the requisite minute quantity of polish. Press it firmly into place as soon as it thickens and rub it level with fine abrasive paper when it is dry. The repair should be permanent and invisible, once polished over.

Opposite: Some wood looks best left in its natural state. Protect the wood with a clear seal.
Right: Some examples of stripped finishes. The settle has been fumed; the cupboard limed; and the chair stripped down to the natural wood.

Grain filling
This is nothing to do with damage, but with the wood's natural grain crevices, which must be filled in before you can varnish a surface. Unless you are to use a polyurethane covering, tint the grain filling compound to match the wood. This can be very tricky, usually involving powder colours ground in oil, so if you feel doubts turn to a transparent grain filler such as that made by Furniglas. However, do not use it under anything other than a polyurethane finish.

Liming
A specialized method of grain filling used to be applied to English oak to bring out the beauty of its grain. Possibly you may have to imitate the process, which consisted in bringing up the grain by wetting and/or wire brushing, scrubbing cream-thick lime solution into the pores with a cloth and rubbing the surface down with abrasive paper after it was dry. Be especially protective of eyes and hands.

Fuming
Another process used on oak was known as fuming; this darkened the wood from its natural light yellow colour. If you have to mend a fumed-oak piece with new wood, you will have to do the fuming before the new component is fitted.

Stand the item in an ammonia-proof drum or container, but do not allow it to touch the concentrated ammonia solution in the bottom. Remember that the chemical attacks some plastics, and that it isn't entirely kind to human beings. All the fumes do to the wood is darken it, so you do not need to bother about residues. Be sure always to work in a well-ventilated room.

STAINS, SEALS AND POLISHES

Very often after you have bleached and filled the wood for your piece, you may like to change the colour by applying a stain of some sort. To prevent any adverse reaction between the stain and a surface finish, try to use a stain which has been recommended by the manufacturer of the surface finish you intend to use.

Whether you have bleached the piece or not, the colour of the wood is bound to affect that of the stain you may want to dye it with. Always consider this when you are choosing colours and make a patch test just to be safe.

Occasionally, you may want to stain only a small area of a piece to match an existing stain. Proprietary matt stains are possible to use for this or you may make up your own stains to the specifications given below.

Mahogany. Bichromate of potash crystals dissolved in water will darken mahogany. Make a concentrated solution and dilute it as required, always testing on a hidden spot before committing yourself. The stain darkens as it dries, so allow the test patch to dry out before proceeding.

Oak. Vandyke crystals dissolved in water with a little ammonia 880 will make an oak stain.

Bismark brown makes a red stain which is useful for warming up other stains.

Black aniline dye is the best for retouching ebony.

To apply the stain, use a soft, dry cloth or a medium-sized brush and apply a coat of the stain evenly over the entire piece. To ensure even colouring, wipe any excess with a clean cloth before the stain dries.

Any kind of stain is safe under oil, but if you want a brilliantly coloured stain water-alcohol borne types, such as those made by Dylon, are the ones to use under modern, chemically curing finishes. All of these dyes are quite simple to use. Remember, however, that they raise grain, so you need to damp surfaces, rub flat with fine abrasive paper when dry and then put the stain on, all *before* you attempt the final surface lacquer or polish.

Surface applications

Before you decide what kind of finish to apply to old wood, consider carefully whether or not its present surface holds any visual or tactile charm that is better preserved than lost.

Transparent varnishes and lacquers are rarely worth leaving, but perhaps you have a piece of furniture that has been finished in the fashion of the pre-French polish era: sealed with linseed oil and repeatedly waxed. This way of protecting a surface is effective for any item unlikely to be subjected to abuse by heat or abrasion and the years of elbow-grease expended on it provide a soft, lustrous patina impossible to replace.

Oiled and waxed finishes

If you plan on conserving such a finish, the prescription is simply more of the same medicine. Take the wax off by rubbing gently with a mineral turpentine substitute on cotton wool; wipe with a dry rag. Finally use linseed oil to reseal the surfaces.

Boiled linseed oil is thicker and more treacly than raw, but you may use either — diluted up to 50/50 with a mineral turpentine substitute if you want to avoid darkening the timber's colour. Even with the diluted oil, you should apply a series of very thin coats with a rag or soft brush, letting each coat dry before putting more on. Continue the oil feeding until the wood will not absorb any more, then rub hard with a clean rag to remove any excess there may be. Use a hard wax, massaged to a shine with grade 000 steel wool to complete the finish.

If you prefer you may use teak oil for this process; it dries quicker than linseed oil and is more resistant to marking.

Resistant finishes

Old wood that has been stripped, perhaps even mildly bleached to remove stains, may still be quite reasonably attractive. To enhance and protect its good looks, you need only give it a careful rub with fine glasspaper and three or four coats of a modern synthetic lacquer.

All transparent finishes darken natural wood to some extent, but if you especially want to avoid any hint of golden brown, use a catalyzed clear lacquer rather than a polyurethane. Lacquers of this kind (Furniglas Hardset is a good example) are just as tough as polyurethanes, but, unlike polyurethanes, cannot be stored once the catalyst has been added. A widely unappreciated feature of catalyzed finishes is that you can put thin, smooth coats on top of basic brush coats with a pad.

Polyurethane practice

Polyurethanes are only as tough as their reputation if they are applied directly to the wood surface — anything coming between may affect their performance. Unlike oils, they will not soak into wood so, to get firm adhesion, dilute the first coat 50/50 with the makers' recommended solvent and the second with 25 per cent solvent. Regard these as a preparation for the three or four full-strength coats necessary. Rub down lightly between coats with 320 or finer grit abrasive paper, or with 000 steel wool.

For a perfect surface

Although modern lacquers can attain an extremely high gloss surface finish by brushing, spraying or pad polishing, there is always the chance of making blemishes with embedded dust or hair — these are almost impossible to avoid with the comparatively long drying time. This is where French polish scores over polyurethanes; its essential quality is the speed at which it sets, drying almost as soon as it leaves the pad, and enabling it to be applied free of inclusions. This very useful virtue has made it traditionally a master craftsman's prerogative to apply — a high degree of skill being needed to get a clean finish, free of smear and bloom.

Two versions of proprietary French polish, such as those made by Furniglas, now overcome this difficulty by means of a special chemical finishing solution. You simply wipe it on after pad polishing, then off again to eliminate those pad marks which used to give apprentices to the trade nightmares.

If you intend to French polish over a polyurethane or catalyzed lacquer, choose a proprietary polyurethane version, but do not attempt to apply this one over ordinary French polish because the under layer of the combined finish will still be heat sensitive. The standard grade is the better one for repairing or reviving the traditional shellac-based finishes. Usually a cleaning fluid is provided to be used with both kinds of polish.

Opposite above: Use natural wood stains to enhance the grain or colour of a piece. Avoid staining woods such as mahogany, walnut or maple. Notice the reflection in the French polished surface of the right hand side of the lower table. Opposite below: Try staining with water-alcohol fabric dyes or artist's inks, as well as normal coloured wood stains.

PAINTING IT PLAIN

Sound, solid and utilitarian though your selected secondhand furniture may be, a high proportion of it is bound to be made from wood with an indifferent surface. Instead of using a clear finish which only produces a disappointing renovation, imagine such pieces straight-painted. They may prove to compare favourably with relatively featureless modern items – whereas if you tried to give them a pretentious finish you might draw attention to their shortcomings.

Superfine painting
Paint is essentially a cosmetic, so to ensure a flawless finish you must have a good foundation. Not too many years ago, it would have been necessary to strip or scrape any surface back to the bare wood, so that you could fill securely and sand finely to get the necessary smooth and unbroken surface. If you have to go to these lengths to get rid of the old finish, any proprietary pre-paint filler will give you an acceptable fair surface to start on. If you have not stripped so thoroughly, the finer fillers close the grain better and may, in the end, save you an extra coat of paint.

Sanding smooth and flat
A thousand laborious ways can be found to get a surface ready for perfectionist painting. One of them is to trowel in a fine filler, then proceed to gouge it out with coarse-grit abrasive paper. All the 60 to 100-grit abrasive work should be done before the filler is put in, leaving as little raised above the surface as possible. Successive rubbings with 150-grit and 320-grit grades will then leave the base you want.

Enemies of adhesion
Before you pick up the paint pot, think back to reassure yourself that no residues are left in the wood which might tend to lift or discolour the new paint film. Possible invisible lurkers are oil, grease, wax, stripping/bleaching/washing compounds, resinous knots and, last but not least, water. Provided you have washed the wood down thoroughly and have allowed it to dry out before filling, only knots should be liable to give trouble; it is always a good idea to seal them off with patent knotting solution and (on softwoods) to use an aluminium primer, which is not the colour of aluminium, but contains a compound of the metal that is very good at resisting the penetration of resin.

More about sanding
Abrasive paper will only cut down bumps on flat sections or remove splinters in hollows if it is supported so that it conforms to the contours of the surface you are working on. Often only your fingertips can be used to hold the paper, although small pieces rolled up can be better to work into narrow flutes and mouldings.

Flat surfaces and edges alike should be block-sanded, the abrasive supported by a flat wooden 'brick', a cork rubbing-pad or a patented hand-sanding holder. If you use special steel-backed sanding sheets, be very careful not to put tucks in them when you fold them into the holder because the resulting corners can make ugly gouge marks.

Power tools
Orbital or rotary-powered sanding tools can be both labour-saving and effective on flat surfaces, but none are really good enough to use on curved parts for fine work. Even with extreme care, flexible disc sanders or attachments for power drills are likely to hollow out a flat section. Instead try using a rigidly backed rotary device or even better, a proper orbital sander. Avoid orbital pads that are not stable. Some simply waggle vigorously around a central pivot, whereas the gentle, scrubbing action of the 'eccentrically' driven kind gives a proper finish.

Without doubt self-powered machines are more effective than attachments for electric drills, because they are made for a single purpose. Either way, it's as well to remember that a sander is a finishing tool and should not be used for heavier work.

There is no point in using any grit coarser than 100 for an orbital pad. Whichever grit you start with, 100 or finer, you will get the best results by working steadily through the available grades up to 320 or 400-grit for the final finish.

Final precautions
Contra-indications are not so much don'ts as nevers: Never add any of your weight (however slight) to that of the sander itself and never cover any of the motor's air vents with either hand. An orbital sander's jobs tend to be long, so the motor needs all the cooling air it can get. Work in slow loops, not straight down the grain, never letting your sander rest with the motor running.

Never tip either end or side when in motion, or allow the pad to touch adjacent walls or ledges. Never stop short of unobstructed edges, nor let the pad project more than an inch or so beyond them.

When you get to the final, finest grade of abrasive paper, carefully and evenly hold the sander as if to lift it bodily straight into the air, but keep it very lightly in contact with the wood.

If you have decided to leave the existing finish on and paint over it, do all but the finest sanding, wipe the dust away and use a spackle (e.g. a cellulose filler, such as Fine Surface Polyfilla) to fill in holes and dents, including those in the old coating. Then fine-sand and proceed to under-coat.

Priming and undercoating
From now on, be clean. Ideally you will have taken off all removable fittings and vacuumed away all dust. Clean the floor while you are at it, close the doors and windows to keep out dust, smoke and insects. If you are a smoker, give it up for safety's sake while you are in the paint room. Wrap up long hair. Leave hairy or woolly clothes in the wardrobe.

To get the best possible paintwork it's worth investing in the best brushes you can afford. Thin, flat, chisel-tip brushes are a great temptation to the inexperienced because they look so manageable. However, when full of paint some of the really inexpensive ones do about as good a job as an old sponge.

The better brushes are fat, with fine, silky bristles that both hold a good charge of paint and spread it out at an even rate. They work with a firm, springy touch like that of an old-fashioned pen nib. The firmness lets you work with the bristle tips.

Between coats
As soon as each coat of paint is thoroughly dry, rub it down with extreme gentleness, using 500 grit, or finer, abrasive paper. In this way you get rid of any odd particles and hairs which may have landed on the surface during drying, and make a sound base for the following top-coats.

With these later coats be as stingy with the paint as it will let you, short of taking it off again. Remove dust between every coat. For heavy-wearing use, substitute an extra gloss topcoat for one of the undercoats.

☐ **Opposite: A few coats of paint can transform any dingy piece into a cheerful addition to the home.**
Above left: Brighten up a nursery by converting an old washstand into a baby's dresser, with a thorough clean inside and out and a colourful painted finish.
Above right: If a bargain piece looks ungainly and drab, strip off the original finish, paint it a brilliant colour and make a feature of its nooks and crannies by lining them with complementary paper or fabric.
Below: Gloss paints are excellent for tables and chairs: they are easy to wipe clean and the paint protects the wood against nicks and scrapes.

DECORATIVE DESIGNS AND STENCILS

For renovators who have found in the process of plain painting that they have a clear eye and a steady hand, contrasting features painted on to an old piece of furniture can completely transform its character. With a bit of planning and imagination, you can make an undistinguished collection of sticks and panels the centre of attention and interest.

Freehand picture patterns

If you make a panel or other chosen section a light coloured oasis in a dark desert of plain paint, the very fact of its colourful existence will draw more attention than any minor imperfections of execution. Pictures on common articles of household furniture are so little encountered, especially on modern furniture designs, that you are far more likely to be congratulated for enterprise than criticized for your specific talents. And moreover, you do not have to be an artistic genius to paint respectable designs. Copying and tracing are both quite legitimate methods of providing yourself with a theme or a shape.

Choosing the paint

Assuming that you start with an object stripped bare of all previous finishes and completely prepared for repainting, you must first decide on the type of paint you want to use. This will enable you to choose the correct primer: aluminium-based ones for softwoods; almost any lead-free type for hardwoods (diluted with a mineral turpentine substitute in the proportions recommended by the manufacturer); and none at all if you are applying a pure polyurethane final finish. The best primer for this type of finish is an eggshell from the same range: dilute the first coat with 50 per cent mineral turpentine substitute and the second with 25 per cent. This will help to make the polyurethane sink into the surface as deeply as possible.

Guide to painting

Let your approach to painting be governed first of all by the contrast between your ground and the pattern or picture background. If the contrast is strong you will probably find it easier to paint the entire object and then superimpose your design onto the background. If there is little contrast, you may prefer to leave a bare wood patch for the design. In this case, when the ground colour is to be brushed or sprayed on, simply mark out the area you need to leave unpainted with chalk or a felt pen and follow the line as closely as you can with a fine brush. Should the area be a complex or difficult shape itself, you may have to trace it from your original. Once you have copied the outline on to your tracing paper, you can shade the underside with a very soft pencil. Put the tracing on to the wood and rub along the lines to press them through.

When the ground colour is to be applied you will need to have some form of protective masking. Self-adhesive vinyl coverings, such as Fablon or Contac, are very effective when stuck on to hardened paint surfaces. They may, however, leave residues on bare wood which will give trouble later. Of course, you can always ensure that no spots of adhesive remain by rubbing the bare patch with a rag moistened with surgical spirit (rubbing alcohol).

Masking solution

Certain types of special 'masking solutions', such as Humbrol's Maskol, have now been specifically developed to eliminate harmful adhesive residues. Painted thinly on the reserved area before you apply the ground, it dries in about 15 minutes to a thin, flexible, rubbery film. If you seal into it a small piece of paper or card, you can peel the protected patch off cleanly when the last spray-coat has dried thoroughly.

Fablon masking precautions

Since PVC coverings (Fablon or Contac) are not designed especially for masking, it is essential that the ground colour is thoroughly hard-dry before putting the mask in place. This means letting alkyd paints dry for at least four days and polyurethanes for a week. An exact shape can be cut with the PVC peel-off backing still in place, leaving you a clean outline with a hard edge to paint around.

Stencilling

For people whose self-confidence and enterprise falls short of attempting original or freehand-copied artwork, there are other ways of bringing life and variety to painted articles.

Stencilling is perhaps the simplest to do, even though the process requires more than average care. Whether you spray or brush through the cutouts, the chief risk is of paint seeping under an unsecured edge.

PVC materials can be used to make stencils, in much the same way as for masking. To prevent the paint from lifting when you remove the self-adhesive material, allow several days for the ground colour to dry before applying the stencil.

Stick-ons and slide-ons

Yet another method of decorating a plain surface is to use any of the ready-made self-adhesive motifs available. They are especially effective on furniture in children's rooms or play-rooms.

Beware, however, that the pictures will be slightly raised from the surface they are applied to and so need careful application to be sure that the edges do not roll up. Occasionally, you will find odd projections on some of these designs, where an animal's tail sticks out for example, so it pays to loosen the figure from its backing all around the edges before you stick it down by the approved method – peeling the backing off gradually as you smooth the design down.

Since the adhesive on the back of most of these motifs is now non-drying, you will find that you can take them off cleanly even after some years. Occasionally you may get a small obstinate patch left on, but this should be easy to remove with surgical spirit (rubbing alcohol) or toluene (a common dye solvent).

Transfers

Supreme thinness is the outstanding virtue of a transfer, which consists of colour printed on to a thin, transparent film which has a water-soluble, gelatinous backing. Although you can slide it about a bit after soaking the backing off and slipping the picture on to the surface, remember that it is fragile and can be pulled apart with the slightest clumsiness. Once in place and dry, however, it becomes part of the surface. A coat of clear, acid-hardening lacquer will protect it.

Opposite: For an imaginative touch, add more than plain colour to your favourite furniture. Above left: A sunny yellow dresser decorated with simple white stars and clouds echoes the wallpaper's colours. Above right: A basic rectangular shape such as this chest looks good with the legs removed and a central front panel painted in an abstract design. Below: Large panelled items are usually ideal for painting in several colours and decorating with repeated patterns.

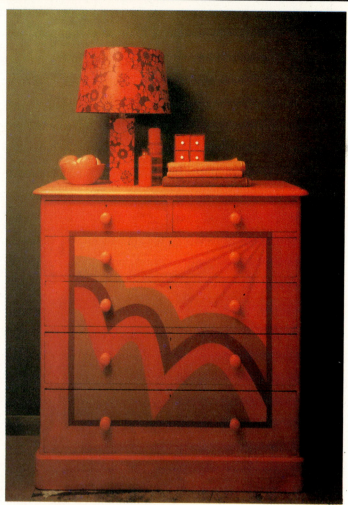

Ideas for design

Inspiration for designs can come from almost anywhere. Nature has always been a source of ideas for pictorial borders and motifs — flowers, animals, patterns, all can be found there. Old books can also be a terrific source of unusual imagery. Some people might find inspiration in needlework patterns as well. And in addition to pictures or designs, consider lettering as an unusual alternative.

Whatever pictures or patterns that you do choose to decorate a plain panel or border edge, be sure that the design is of a similar, compatible style to the piece of furniture. For example, delicate curves and bold regular, geometric patterns are, as a rule, not a good mixture. Also be sure that the size of your design is in proportion to the area that you are painting on. As a final precaution, keep in mind the use to which you are going to put the object.

Colour sense

As with all techniques for renovating furniture, the inexperienced should always try out their ideas first to be sure that they work. Colour combinations are no exception. Probably the most important thing to remember is that complementary colours will enhance one another — to make a colour more prominent put it next to its complement (blue-orange, yellow-purple, red-green). Also any glaze which is put on to a painted surface will usually soften the colours.

Stripes

Plain stripes are the most effective treatment for certain types of furniture. You will find that they are easiest to apply if you use a flat, narrow brush, or even better one of the brushes specially made for striping (ask at your local art supply shop or a good DIY shop).

When painting, be sure that the paint is thin enough to flow easily from the brush and that you put plenty of paint on it. Let the brush move along smoothly: little pressure from your hand is needed. If you lift the brush up in the middle of the stripe it is almost certain to show. Once again, practice will be the best instructor. A straight-edge is always a useful guide to keep handy. If you are doing corner stripes, make the lines go just beyond the corner point and wipe off the excess immediately. Work carefully and at a fairly quick pace — too slow and the shakes will show.

Experiment

Besides design and colour you might try experimenting a bit with special effect paints, such as glitter or metallic paints. Be sparing with their application, as a touch is usually enough to create the desired look.

For unusual textures you might also try applying one of the many coloured glazes now on the market, with feathers, rough cloth or paper.

Freehand techniques

Only a fortunate few will be able to paint an original design directly on to the wood surface. Less gifted people will need help to make their imaginative visions look reasonably proficient. Perhaps the most helpful and encouraging way to show what can be achieved by tracing and copying, will be to describe how the rocking chair and sea-chest were done.

The Boston rocker

If there is any golden rule for design painting, it is to wait until the initial colour is bone-hard dry before proceeding to the next one. This is exactly how a watercolourist works to avoid blurred outlines.

Both the white ground and the tan border around the design on the chair were painted using PVC masks. The leaf shapes were achieved by tracing around a pattern with a piece of chalk and then painting in with fine, sable brushes. For almost any painted design work, sable brushes are the best to use. They have finely pointed

tips and round, seamless, non-corrodible ferrules. Sizes are denoted by numbers, each number relating to the diameter at the narrow end of the ferrule which holds the soft bristles. They range from No. 1 at 1·65mm to No. 10 at 6·45mm, so any fine work you need to do can be completed with a brush appropriate to the job. Without proper brushes, you do not give yourself a reasonable chance of success.

All veins and shading in the leaves were painted with a No. 3 brush – the veins in black enamel, diluted with a lot of mineral turpentine substitute

(proportions not critical) and the shading with the same brush but an even more dilute mixture of the colour.

Sea-chest design
One or two fatter pencils proved useful in the creation of the ship picture but no great art was involved. Since the imprecise rope border had been planned before the centre panel was painted, the panel outline was traced instead of masked. After priming the bare wood, the complete ship was traced on to it.

Sky was stippled in, then the green middle tint of the sea. The hull needed

a little reinforcement with a 7B pencil before it was painted in, and then the masts and sails were added.

Shading with a mixture of cream and white came next, then the darker green of the sea, the ropes and other fine details before the final 'white horses' and rope border.

Opposite above: A sea-chest design for a blanket box. To get the best effects, mix colours. Opposite below: Simple shapes can be traced on with everyday household templates. Above: A unique Boston rocker.

This page : Designs for the Boston rocker, the Tyrolean chest, the sea chest and an appealing rag doll for a child's room, are given as a guide for making accurate tracings and stencils. To enlarge a design from a small original, simply trace it up on a squared graph drawn to the scale of the proposed picture.

If using stencils, hold them firmly in place with masking tape; provide extra borders if using an aerosol spray paint. Test the masking tape on an unnoticeable area of a pre-painted base to be sure it does not pull off the paint.

PAINTING DIFFICULT SURFACES

Man-made boards make very sound replacements for tops too senile for renovation, but their edges may give rise to some trouble unless they are properly treated. Both blockboard and plywood edges show end grain, which absorbs paint to a greater extent than the rest of the wood. If you apply a thick coating of a cellulose filler, let it dry and then rub it down finely, the board's structure will become a close secret, after painting.

Chipboard edges should really be lipped with some smooth material for the best results, but the same treatment works quite well for their raw edges, too. Chipboard has a very abrasive texture, especially at the edges, which tends to tear abrasive paper, even if it is wrapped around a block. Steel-backed abrasive sheets, such as those supplied for some types of hand sanders are one solution to this problem.

Finally, unless you have one of the extra-fine surfaced chipboards, you will find that the broad surfaces need a certain amount of filling as well before you can paint them satisfactorily.

Spackling sound paint
Paradoxically, until recently dents and bruises in sound paintwork could be too shallow to fill, and so more difficult to hide than deep gouges or splits. Adhesive spackles, such as the vinyl-based Fine Surface Polyfilla, have changed all this. They are fine-textured enough to sand flush to the edges of the most gently undulating depression in painted wood (or painted anything). An additional advantage is that they need no primer, as they do not have the same tendency as ordinary filler to soak up the undercoat.

Painting plastics
Plastics are so many in kind and so various in character that it is nearly impossible to state rules of thumb concerning the sort of paint which can safely be used on any particular one. Any given plastic may react to a paint quite differently in one form than it does to the same paint when it has been made by a different method. Generally speaking, hard plastics can usually be painted safely with products that use a mineral turpentine substitute as their solvent. The only reliable guide to test the stability of the partnership is to try a little paint on an unobtrusive part of the plastic. Polyurethane paints are among the safest to try, and some spray paints, such as Humbrol aerosols, are safe to use even on expanded polystyrene.

Above: Plastic surfaces can be given striking new looks although they do present some difficulties for the painter. Always experiment beforehand to find the right paint: one which will not eat into the surface. Remember to plan ahead for matching designs and use masking tape or templates for accuracy.

THE KNACK OF APPLYING 'FAKE' FINISHES

Paints and surface finishes may be used to achieve effects which in no way resemble ordinary paintwork. If you are unable to find, or to afford, one of the more unusual types of material such as marble, malachite, ebony or a beautifully grained wood, it is possible to emulate them quite easily, with paint and paintbrush.

Sometimes the effect can be quite startling — and often pleasantly surprising. It is an especially good technique to use on fairly small or oddly shaped items which would be quite charming, except for their dull finish. A bit of practice and a good eye can produce imitations of expensive timbers, marbles or malachite which will deceive all but the expert. The main reason for applying faked finishes is, of course, to brighten an object's appearance by giving it an original surface, rather than to deceive.

The basics of deception
Whether you are graining to imitate wood or veining to imitate minerals, the basic technique is the same. First, a ground colour in an oil-based paint is put on and allowed to dry very well. A thin coat of linseed oil is applied on to this ground, using a soft pad to wipe it over, and various combinations of paint, or stain. Features can be added in two ways: either by removing part of the overlay or by painting them in with small brushes. Finally the design is sealed in with a clear varnish.

The most difficult aspects are getting the colours right and putting the features in, but with a little practice, any reasonably steady hand can produce quite effective results. The indispensable part of the process is a careful study of the material you are trying to recreate. If you cannot have it in front of you while you work, at least go and look at it for a good long time before you start.

For clear varnishing, acid-catalyzed lacquers, such as Furniglas Hardset, are better than polyurethanes. They do not have the slight brown tinge that is inseparable from the polyurethanes (fine for natural wood; death to light shades of paint).

The art of ebonizing
To give wood a solid, dense black appearance, with no grain figure visible whatsoever, you can use either a proprietary French polish preparation or a catalyzed lacquer to which you add black powder colour especially formulated for the job. Use the proportions recommended by the makers, allowing several hours for the colour to dissolve. If the lacquer is a two-solution, catalyzed lacquer you need to add the hardener to the blackened lacquer just before using it.

Several brush coats go on before you start to pad-polish (preferably wearing rubber gloves). In this operation, you can have the best of both worlds by pad-polishing over the brush-coated lacquer with the blackened French polish preparation. If you do this, the surface will be easy to repair if it is scratched or dented. At the same time you will retain the heat and solvent protection of the base layers of catalyzed lacquer.

Graining the hat boxes
Even if you are only having fun with imitation surfaces, the effect would be marred by edges out of line or pronounced dents in the surfaces. The first priority in graining the hat boxes shown was to knock out the depressions and straighten up the edges. For both operations, the *light* hammering was done against a firm wood backing of appropriate shape.

After cleaning and degreasing with steel wool and a mineral turpentine substitute, the tinplate was given two undercoats, Marders Matsire MU2 for the pine coloured box and MU4 for the rosewood one.

The next application is a very thin layer of oilpaint over a darker one, which is known as scumble. This was thinned down to the right shade with a two-to-one mixture of a mineral turpentine substitute and raw linseed oil, and was put on extremely thinly. All the grain lines were done with fine sable brushes, but if you can get any of the special graining tools the job will be even quicker and easier.

Large art supply firms still make pencil overgrainers for the annual-ring lines, mottlers which dig through scumble to make fine highlights, floggers for suggesting pores and softeners to blend the sharp lines a little and so reduce the artificiality.

Polyurethane varnish will not be as hard-wearing over the oil-based graining as it would be on its own, but it is still the best protection available.

Opposite: The grained boxes were done with artist's paints; the malachite box was painted with household paints and given two coats of a clear polyurethane finish tinted with green stain. Malachite and marble patterns shown below.

CANE FURNITURE

Bamboo is a giant grass plant, whereas rattan and malacca are slender stems from different kinds of palm tree. All are sometimes referred to as 'cane', to complete our confusion.

In practical terms this is of little consequence, because they all have rather similar characteristics. The difference between ordinary, tree-grown woods and the endogenous woody stems of the 'canes' is that, instead of forming new tissue on the outside as they grow, grasses and palms make their new growth on the inside. Notwithstanding this peculiar habit, endogens, of course, must have hollow stems. For this reason, they present us with hard, horny material on the outside, but with little or nothing on the inside to take screws, nails or any of the usual carpentry-orientated fastening devices.

Which is used for what
Although technically a grass, bamboo is normally used for furniture in a thicker and sturdier state of development than that made from palm stems such as rattan. The reason for this is that its segments tend to be longer, linked by rather knotty joints. Palms, on the other hand, have shorter, less irregular segments, with neater and smoother joins between them, which allow them to bend more readily into curves.

Problems in the spring
Although malacca (a favourite for walking-style canes) and rattan are ready to bend, they are equally ready to spring back straight again as soon as they are released from tension. When load-bearing furniture is made from these materials, this resilience has to be used to provide the resistance to deformation that solid timber gives through its natural stiffness.

By far the most usual method of fastening stems together is to bind them with thin strips of fibrous reed or cane. The binding strips will have been soaked in water to make them conform to the tight curves required in lashing rattan members together. Once in place and tied off (normally by being tucked under), the strips harden and become brittle.

Dealing with disintegration
Palm-built furniture very rarely comes apart because of longitudinal splits in the cane structural pieces. More often than not it is the bindings that break their bands and demand attention

before the entire piece collapses.

Two problems arise when this happens. The original bindings cannot be re-used, and the bent members show a reluctance to go back to their original form. They, like the bindings, tend to increase in brittleness with age, so you may not be able to heave them into position quite so enthusiastically as the original maker did. A pan full of boiling water can work wonders in this situation. Be sure, however, that the water can drain away and that you can get the recalcitrant rod into place and lashed down before it again becomes set in its ways. 'Peastick' bamboo or split cane is best to use for any binding.

Bigger bamboos
Furniture made from the fatter and thicker walled bamboos may be held together by methods other than binding. To repair items that have been notched or pinned is perhaps easier than bandaging up the lashed-construction kind, because the big-diameter poles can, with care, be drilled — with care meaning with a power drill and a proper wood auger. Ordinary twist bits for drills tend to split the bamboo walls, as do hand auger bits, which have a screw-threaded point.

Screws can even be used, although you might need to fill part of a hollow stem with cellulose filler, such as Polyfilla, or one of the resin fillers used for repairing minor damage on car bodies. If you use the latter, it is advisable to drill it after it has set, inserting a masonry plug to give the screw a solid hold. Always drill at a slow speed to avoid splits and fractures.

Camouflaging the repair

It is inadvisable to bury screw heads below the bamboo surface, since you will need the full thickness of the wall to stop the screw from pulling through. If you must leave the screw flush with the surface, it can easily be disguised by a dab of paint.

Most of the repairs to bamboo or rattan furniture will, however, be rebinding jobs. Original strips will almost never be serviceable enough to be used again. And substitutes like plastic, string or plastic-covered wire can be disguised only by painting, fortunately a very effective rejuvenation treatment for this kind of furniture and one with a variety of possibilities.

Painting peculiarities

Whether laced together or notched and spiked, cane-constructions are bound to present more complex surfaces to be cleaned and painted than solid wood ones. For this reason, avoid powdery scouring compounds. Rely rather on strong-action liquid detergents, which can more reliably be washed out from the interstices and crannies. Pre-paint preparations are most effective, and can normally be let down to thinner solutions for simply lifting dirt. If you do intend painting or varnishing, use them at the recommended full strength.

Some pieces will respond to gentle cleaning with an old paintbrush, but others may need the stiffer persuasion of a scrubbing brush, for example. Sanding is naturally out of the question for all but the broadest bamboos, so it will help a lot if you can find a cleaner with an etching action thrown in to give paint a good key.

Above: Bamboo and rattan are remarkably versatile: cane chairs, tables, even chests of drawers, bring an interesting touch of the orient to a living room or bedroom. Liven up a narrow hallway with a spiky bamboo hallstand. Use an aerosol spray paint for awkward shapes and fine struts, or clean the cane and varnish it to show off its natural grain and colour.

While repairs to cane furniture such as bamboo and rattan may sometimes be awkward and the results uncertain, complete recaning of a simple chair seat or screen is a project well worth the effort. Even pieces with little or no value can be converted into attractive, useful additions to your home.

Buying cane

Cane can be bought at most craft or DIY shops and usually comes in bundles large enough to cover a small chair seat. There are six thicknesses identified by number. A normal-sized chair seat should be covered with grade four cane. Finishing work on the chair will require a small amount of grade two cane.

Preliminary steps

If you are recaning a damaged chair or article, begin by stripping off the old cane and discarding any pegs or nails which have been used to jam pieces of cane into the holes.

If you are caning a chair frame for the first time, you will need to drill holes for the cane. It is very important for the frame to be level all the way around. The holes must be drilled at the same spacing all round the frame — except where corners make this impossible. The centre front hole must line up exactly with the centre rear one and the side holes must line up exactly across the frame. Since chair frames are wider at the front than at the back, there will be more holes at the front, but this is not a problem.

For grade four cane, use a 3·00mm ($\frac{1}{8}$-inch) drill bit. Space the holes at 15mm ($\frac{1}{2}$-inch) between centres.

Clean out all holes — old or new — with a very fine wire or stick. Failure to do this may mean that the cane will stick. Also give the frame a quick wipe over with a mineral turpentine substitute and polish it if necessary.

Finally soak the cane to be used in cold water for at least five minutes so that it is pliable enough to work with. Repeat this while caning, if it becomes stiff.

Tools

The only tools you will need are three or four blunt pegs, made from thin dowels, to jam into the holes and hold the cane firm, and a razor blade.

Weaving the cane

Carefully study the weaving diagram at every stage of work. Begin with one strand of the softened cane, sharpened at both ends with the razor blade. Find the centre back and front holes and insert one end of the cane through the centre back hole, leaving about 25mm (1 inch) protruding below the underside of the frame. Jam a wooden peg into this hole to hold the cane firmly. Take the other end of the cane across to the centre front hole and push it through the hole from above. Be sure not to twist the cane; keep the shiny side upwards.

Pull the free end of the cane down through the frame so that it does not sag across the chair. Do not pull it too taut, since the cane will shrink as it dries. Pull the cane up through one of the holes adjacent to the centre front

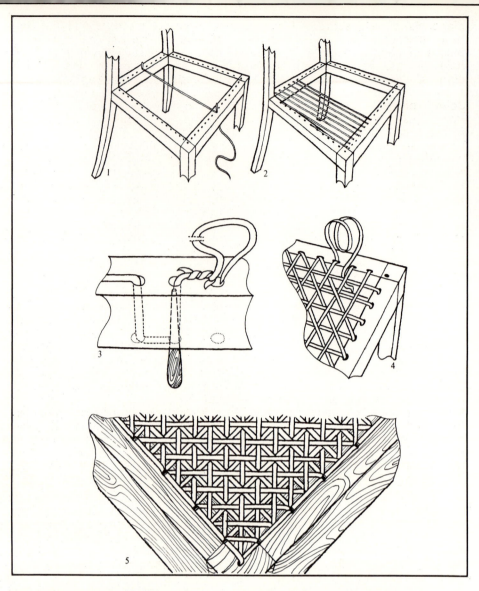

1. Begin caning from a hole at the back of the frame and secure the cane with a peg as shown.
2. With more holes in the front than the back, some strands will run from the front to a side hole.
3. Join a new length by looping it around the old and pulling it tight up through the next hole.

4. Diagonal canes must be interwoven with existing strands. After caning diagonally in one direction, apply the same method in the other.
5. Follow this weaving pattern for the seat at every stage. Figure 3 shows how the cane is passed from hole to hole.

one and back across the frame to the opposite hole, next to the centre back one. Continue to insert parallel strands across the top of the frame, joining lengths of cane as described below, until you reach the last hole before one of the rear corners.

Corners

Since there are more holes in the front than the back of the frame some strands will have to run from the front to a side hole. Be sure to place the strands so that they are kept exactly parallel to one another. When you have finished one side, return to the centre of the frame and work out to the other side; be sure to do both sides exactly the same.

Side to side

Begin at the front of the frame and string the cane from side to side. Lay the side to side canes over the front to back ones to provide a frame for the diagonally woven strands.

Diagonal strands

Study the weaving diagram carefully at every stage. Begin at either rear corner and pass the strand of cane over and then under the first two intersections of the strung cane. This will make the angle 45° to either of the first two sets of cane. String right across the frame to the corner, passing above and below alternate intersections. String the next diagonal piece of cane opposite to this one (over where you went under) and continue alternating each strand. Finish the weaving by stringing across the other diagonal, passing the strand below the intersections that the previous diagonals passed above. When you have finished, there will be three pieces of cane through each of the holes in the frame, except at the corners.

Joining pieces

Remember, when you are joining pieces of cane that it can only be done under the frame on the short stretch where the cane passes from one hole to another. Pass the first cane down through its hole and hold it firm at the top with a peg. Then loop, do not knot, the new piece around the protruding end, right up against the frame. Sharpen both ends of the new piece of cane and pass it up through its hole. Pull it tight and the looped link should jam up against the frame. This joint will hold when the cane dries. Remove pegs when a second piece of cane is passed through a hole.

Finishing off

When the cane dries, it shrinks in its holes and, therefore, may slip when a person sits on the seat. This can be avoided by the use of a cane reinforcement made of grade two cane. Begin with this thinner piece of cane and pass it up a frame hole from the underside.

Loop the piece around the three strands coming out of the top of the hole, and pass it down through the same hole. Then, take this piece along the underside of the frame to the next hole and repeat the procedure. This should be done all around the frame, joining up new lengths as previously described.

Finally, the edge of the seat may be decorated with more cane, preferably of a thick grade such as number six, threaded all around the edge of the frame in straight lines from hole to hole, as shown in the weaving diagram. To cover all the spaces between the holes you will need to go around the frame twice.

Basketweave and wickerwork

Though essentially different from furniture made from cane components lashed together, wickerwork constructions produce similar problems if they are badly broken. In fact, it would be wise to reconsider before buying a severely damaged item because any repairs will inevitably involve reweaving.

Most basketwoven pieces are made of thin under-and-over lacings which connect, position and support the basic framework of thicker twigs.

These thin bindings are not too difficult to replace, but the thicker 'ribs' are extremely difficult — if not impossible — to replace. Avoid taking on any furniture with these 'ribs' smashed or split.

Tough and aged bindings will probably demand cutting tools much stronger than scissors. Plier-type snips or garden pruners are both good. New bindings are soaked in water to make them supple before they are laced in.

Painting and varnishing

Brushing paint on to any kind of woven or bound structure is quite a laborious process and for such items spray painting is by far the best technique to use.

A decent aerosol will contain as much as 400 grammes (about 14 ounces) of paint, enough to cover a good-sized chair twice over. The golden rule for all spray painting is to put on thin coats, and allow plenty of drying time in between, until you produce the required finish.

Below: The natural cane chairs add a friendly touch to this bedroom setting. Notice the cleverly arranged frames for displaying favourite pictures.

EASY RE-UPHOLSTERY FOR CHAIR SEATS

The development of foam and other modern materials has made upholstery much easier for the amateur, although time and patience are still essential.

Foam padding principles

Begin with an absolutely firm foundation for the tacks, filling in old tack-holes with slivers of hardwood rather than knife-in fillers. Err (if at all) on the generous side when deciding how many webbing strands to put in: it's the easiest job of all, and all the work you do after is wasted if the foundation sags. Smooth off any roughness wherever covers are to be stretched over edges.

Above all, pull down foam edges evenly. A pair of upholsterer's pliers helps enormously with this: they have square-looking, flat jaws which grip a fair width very firmly. Of course, you do not have to pull at the foam itself. Instead, this must always have un-bleached calico strips stuck to the edges whenever pulling or stretching is necessary. More details are given below.

Pincushion padding

This method of upholstering a seat produces the neatest appearance when it is used on a previously cane-bottomed chair, which will have a shallow rebate around the edge. The bottom of such a chair may or may not still be sound enough to hold tacks. If it is, the webbing is tacked down into it, stopping about $\frac{1}{4}$ inch (6mm.) short of the rebate side to allow room for the anchorage of the foam pad and the cover.

Cut 1-inch (25mm.) foam to the shape of the rebate, but $\frac{1}{4}$ inch smaller all around. Then trim its edges with scissors so that they are bevelled at an angle less than 45°. Now stick calico strips to the foam edges, 2 inches wide (51mm.) and two to a side. These are used together to pull and to hold the foam in place so that the bevel is forced down to make a gently curved finish.

Before you tack the foam down, stick fill-in pieces of webbing into the spaces which separate the support strips. This will help to prevent un-sightly ripples. Drive in the tacks very precisely along the line where foam edge meets chair. This is hard to do but vital, (a one-handed punch helps).

Having cut off all the spare calico, you can fit the cover. The nailing sequence when doing this is very

important. Be sure to fit all tacks loosely into position before driving any of them home.

First spike the middle of each side, then the front edge, working out from the centre to within an inch or two of each corner. The back row is next, then each side in turn. Cut back the cover-piece to project to a reasonable hem-width beginning from the tack lines. This hem may be almost negligible if the material is thick, but it is still better to turn it under. Do this by lifting out all the tacks, a side at a time, and putting them in again (for the last time) after turning the hem under. Do not forget to snip away excess thickness at the corners.

Damaged chair bottoms

Where a rebate is too lacerated to take more tacks, tack the webbing up to the underside of the chair frame and fill in the extra depth with additional foam. In very bad cases you may then have to anchor the remaining upholstery to the wooden strip outside the rebate.

Opposite: This simple wooden chair has been turned into an impressive feature for any room, with a few coats of paint and a simple-to-make seat cover and cushion in a dramatic floral print.

Drop-in chair seats

1. With the cut edge of the webbing facing in, tack it down with 3 tacks in a triangle. Turn the webbing over and tack again with 3 tacks in a reverse triangle.
2. Stretch the webbing across to the front of the frame using a strainer.
3. Tack the webbing again with 3 tacks. Leave an inch spare after cutting and turn this back over the first tacks. Fix with 3 tacks in a reverse triangle. Do the same for each piece.
4. Copy the webbing pattern on the original upholstery where possible.
5. Cover the webbing with hessian, tacking it to the frame ½ inch from the edge of the fabric. Tack these raw edges down.
6. Place tape at each edge of the foam as shown.
7. Place the foam on the hessian and tack the free edge of the tape to the frame. As the foam is larger than the frame it will form a dome.
8. For the cover: make a double pleat at the corners and tack the centre point. Fold the excess fabric into pleats and tack. Cut off excess fabric and cover the seat bottom with a piece of linen. Fold under all raw edges and tack.

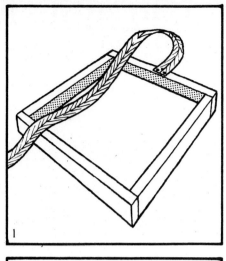

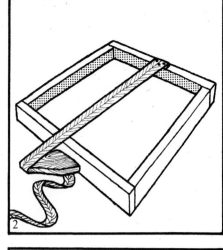

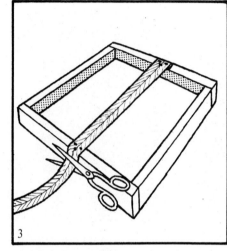

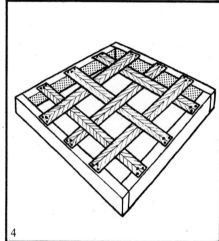

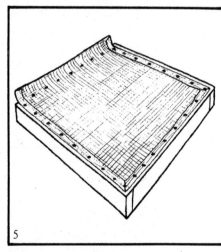

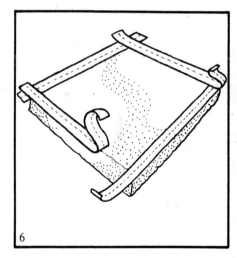

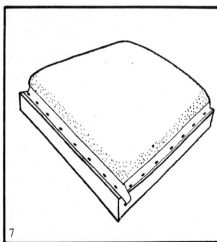

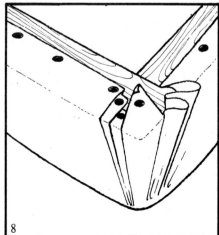

SPRUNG UPHOLSTERY

Button Chesterfields are still one of the most elegant furniture styles, and beautifully finished ones are usually quite expensive. It is possible, however, to buy a shabby old Chesterfield (not necessarily buttoned) at a low price and to re-cover it for a fraction of the cost you would pay for a new one.

A few precautions
While a complete novice should not begin upholstering on a button Chesterfield it is perfectly feasible for someone with a bit of experience to attempt. Competence in buttoning and pleating is important—and patience is particularly necessary. This project may take you over a month to complete, but do not rush or try to invent any short cuts. The techniques given here are applicable to all seating that is sprung and filled.

Stripping down
Strip the sofa down to the bare wood frame, removing every tack and scrap of fabric. Fill in any holes with plastic wood and rub them down with abrasive paper once the filler has dried. Make any other repairs to joints, etc, and treat the frame for woodworm if necessary. (Do this last so as not to affect any adhesive you may need to use.) After treating for woodworm, allow the frame to dry for at least a week.

Back and side fillings
Follow the step-by-steps for lashing the springs and filling the seat with the coconut fibre. Do the same for the back and arms, and cover with the light canvas. Tack the canvas in place along all edges except the arm fronts. At this point the fabric is stitched as shown in the drawings and the filling is tied to the 'sandwich' canvases.

Button preparation
Mark out the planned positions of the buttons on the light canvas. With the scissors cut a diagonal 1½-inch (35mm.) slit where each button will be placed. Open out the filling by clearing a 'shaft' 1¼ inches in diameter through each slit. Do this by inserting the flat end of the regulator through the slit and forcing the filling away from the slit all the way down to the base canvas. This will allow the buttons to sink deeply.

The top cover patterns
Ten pieces of fabric are needed for the cover – a front border panel, seat, inside and outside back, two inside

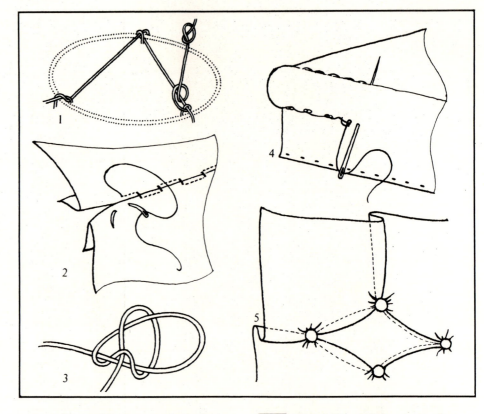

arms, two outside arms and two facing panels for the arms. To work out the dimensions of each piece, measure the length and width of each of the above areas, then add 4 inches (100mm) to each measurement to account for the filling and buttoning. Transfer the final dimensions to a sheet of cheap muslin and cut out. These pieces are placed over the final filling to check that the pattern fits, and are then used to outline the cutting for the final covers.

The final covering
Once you have cut out the final cover you can proceed to stitch it in place. The seat cover is lockstitched along the front edge, stretched over the filling, compressing the horsehair to 1 inch (25mm), and tacked in place along the back and sides. The back, arms, and front panel are done in the same way, but with these panels the buttons must be placed and secured and the material pleated before the fabric is tacked down. The arms are pleated in 'rays' before tacking down. Stitch and tack all remaining covers in place.

Buttoning
To place the buttons, thread a needle and push the eye of it (an upholstery needle is pointed at both ends) through the outside cover and through the shaft in the coconut fibre. When

Opposite: With care and patience you can transform a dowdy, old-fashioned sofa into an elegant, fashionable button-back.
Above: 1. Method for securing the springs to the webbing, and the canvas to the tops of the springs.
2. A slip-stitch, used to fasten the light canvas over back and side fillings.
3. A slip-knot, used for pulling the buttons down.
4. The front edge of the seat being stitched in a roll.
5. A pleating detail.

the eye of the needle has just pierced the base canvas, place a 1-inch scrap of webbing between the twine and the needle. This will act as an anchor and prevent the twins from pulling through the canvas.

Pull the other end of the needle back through the canvas, cut through the main cover, and secure the twine tight so that the slip knot forces the button into the filling. Leave the ends loose with about a 4-inch (100mm.) loose end. When all buttons are fitted, knot each length of twine, cut the loose ends to ½ inch and tuck under the button (see diagrams).

As each button is sunk into position, the fabric is pleated out to take up the excess material. The front panel is pleated vertically, and the back and side ones are diamond pleated.

Essential tools and materials:
Tools you will need are: a mallet
with a 100mm or 4 inch head, a
ripping chisel for removing tacks,
a 6 ounce claw or Warrington
hammer, a webbing stretcher,
heavy duty scissors (230mm or
9 inches), a curved spring needle, a
heavy straight needle (250mm or
10 inches long) for the main
stitching, a light straight needle
(250mm) for buttoning, a small
curved needle (75mm or 3 inches)
for finishing edge joints.
Materials you will need are
(quantities vary with the size of the
unit): webbing to anchor the springs
at the base, springs, heavy canvas
(about 12 ounces), light canvas or
scrim (about 7½ ounces), coconut
fibre for the first stuffing, horsehair
for the 'top' filling, upholstery
wadding, upholstery tacks, 3-ply
sisal cord for lashing the springs,
flax twine for stitching and
buttoning, cover fabric and a
quantity of buttons pre-covered in
matching fabric.

1. With the frame upside down
secure the webbing across the
bottom rails. Begin with strips
running from back to front.
After tacking each strip at the rear,
use the stretcher to pull the
webbing across the frame and
hold it while 4 securing nails are
driven in.
2. When the webbing has been
stretched across the frame in a
basketweave pattern, the frame
is turned right side up and the
springs are stitched down with the
curved spring needle.
3. The springs are compressed
about 35mm (1½ inches) and kept
in place by knotting sisal along the
tops and securing at the outer edges
of the frame.
4. When the seat springs have been
compressed and tied, heavy canvas
is laid over and nailed to the frame
rails. Work from back to front to
sides. Then stitch the canvas to the
tops of the springs as shown on the
previous page.
5. The positioning for the arm and
back springs: the lashing is only
carried out horizontally.
6. Lay 102mm (4 inches) of coconut
fibre over the seat and cover with
light canvas so the fibre is
compressed about 35mm.
7. Tack the light canvas along the
back and side rails and stitch it
along the front as shown on the
previous page. Then anchor the
filling between the two canvases
as shown.
8. Cut diagonal slits for the buttons
and clear the fibre stuffing down to
the base canvas.
9. Horsehair stuffing is placed over
the second seat canvas. Anchor
strands of twine to the canvas and
pull them up through the stuffing.

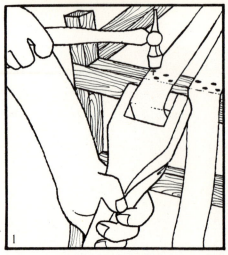

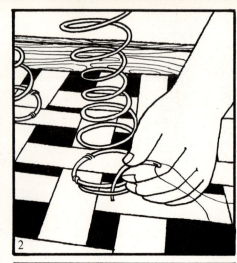

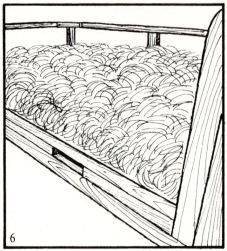

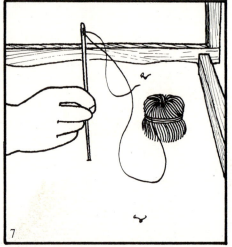

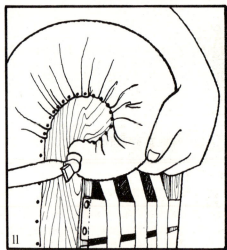

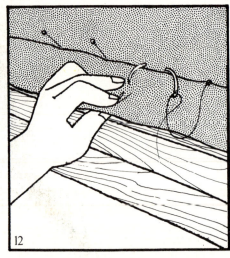

10. Next, lay wadding over the
horsehair and stitch the anchored
twine through it. The wadding
stops bits of stuffing protruding
through the cover.
11. This shows the pleating and
fitting procedure for the front of the
arms. Pay particular attention to
this point – it acts as a mould for
the final cover.
12. Laying the final canvas over the
seat. Skewers or pins hold the
material in place while it is being
stitched.
13. Pulling the button through. The
line at the opposite end is anchored
to the base canvas by a scrap roll of
webbing.

14. Pleating and buttoning. These
are done together to accommodate
the quantity of loose material.
15. Pleating the final cover around
the front edges of the arm rest.
The nails in the middle are covered
with a separate panel of
material.
16. Running the skirting panel
along the front. When stitched,
the material is pleated down and
nailed under the rail.
17. Fitting the top seat panel.
This is stitched along the front,
pleated over to the back and nailed
along the back.
18. Stitching the arm cover panel
in place.

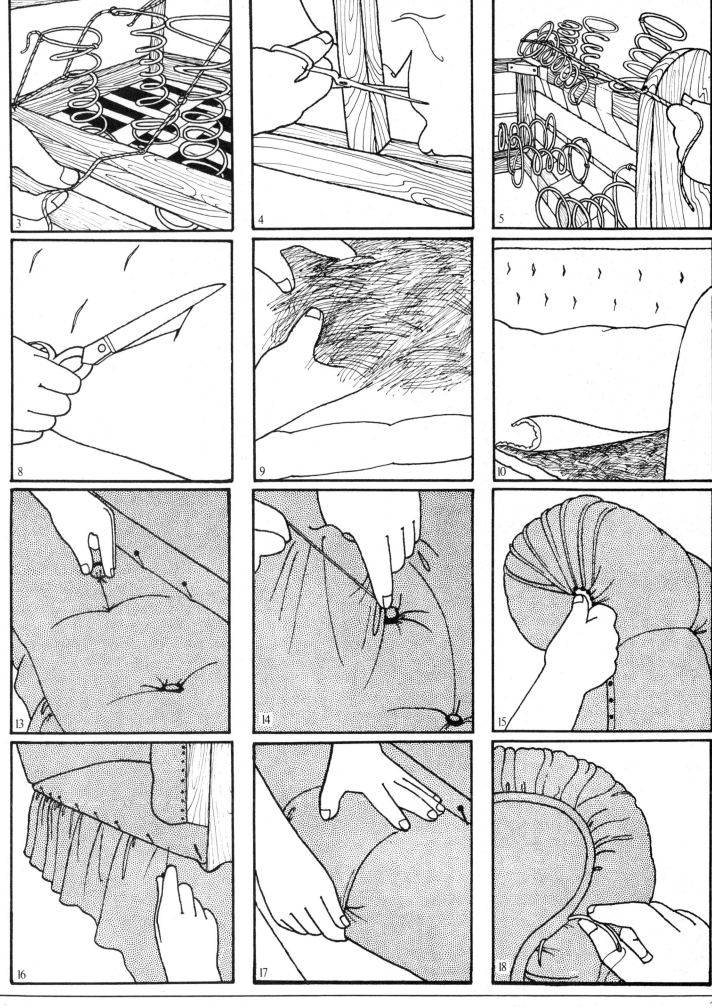

THE LOOK OF LEATHER

Real leather in new condition is almost impossible to distinguish from man-made imitations, some of which are good enough to deceive experts, if only outside their laboratories.

The older it gets, however, the more its advantages over the plastics become apparent, if it's been looked after. If it hasn't, the more its short-comings will become evident.

Features to look for

As it grew originally on an animal, a hide naturally has a grain (running from nose to tail) and pores (all over). Invariably it is smoother on the outside than on the inside. Different animals produce different grades of leather, as do older or younger beasts of the same kind, and so do different parts of the same hide.

Unless hide is tanned to convert it into leather, it simply rots away – something it can still do eventually if its surface is allowed to crack and its softer layers to absorb water. In this condition, leather is prey to moulds and fungi which cause its layers to separate.

This separation is what to look for in secondhand leather-covered furniture. If it's disintegrating, don't imagine there's anything you can do to save it. Even in the sorriest state, it may cost you heavily to buy it, and a total re-covering job will dwarf that expenditure.

Cosmetic colour

Damage to the leather surface caused by cutting, tearing or burning may be quite extensive, but not enough to affect the overall soundness of a piece. In these circumstances, any one of a number of proprietary paints, polishes or colouring compounds can very effectively restore its respectability. Popular motoring magazine advertisements are a good source for renovating paints, and women's magazines for shoe-colourings. Neither will do its best for you if the leather is very greasy, so wipe it over with methylated spirit on a rag before you start.

Feeding and maintenance

Upholsterers and leather-goods shops usually stock a thick white cream called 'Hide Food'. This should be used regularly for cleaning and polishing leather furniture, once you have it in reasonable condition. Good advice normally offered on the jar is 'little and often'. Take it.

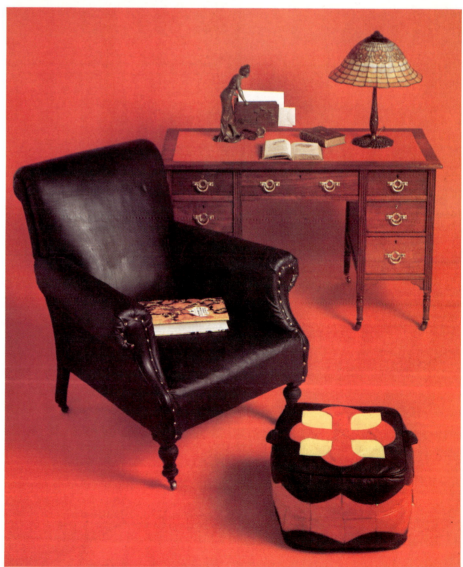

Opposite: The before and after looks of leather-covered furniture: for large recovering jobs, some of the man-made vinyls will provide superb results – and at an economical price.

Patching a tear

A split will very probably have appeared along the grain of the leather, as a result of some sharp object or corner penetrating a panel. Catch it soon after it has been done and the problem is less because there isn't likely to be any loss of leather, or panel deformation. A small patch should, then, do the trick.

Short tears and long tears

Short tears are far easier to patch, since the panel they appear in isn't likely to have lost tension and you will still have a fairly firm ground to apply your patch to. With a longer rip you may have the twin problems of floppy edges and lack of easy access behind to enable you to bring the torn edges together, even temporarily, without recourse to stitching. Unless you can release one or two sides of the panel to secure the loose edges from the back, you may have to loop them together with twine.

Considerable strength may be demanded of a patch if it is to hold a long tear securely, so allow a generous area for the adhesive to get a grip on either side of the tear and at each end. A patch's permanence will depend on the area covered, on the strength of the bond and on the character of the adhesive. Strongest of all are the epoxy resin types, now on the market in quick-setting forms, which make *ad hoc* jobs like leather patching possible.

Although the bond given by epoxies is extremely strong, it is not flexible, so on panels which are liable to flexing strains it might be better to use a less durable but more flexible contact adhesive. Almost any will be suitable for leather-to-leather joins.

No matter what the adhesive you use, in any situation, and no matter what surfaces you are joining, failure of the bond is almost a certainty unless you thoroughly de-grease the areas. Leather is more likely than most materials to hold traces of grease, oil or wax, so take a little extra trouble to make sure of removing all traces.

Smooth edges for patches

When you buy a bicycle puncture repair kit, you will usually find that the patches are chamfered off to a feather edge, so that they will not catch on the outer tyre as you reinstall the tube. When patching leather furniture, you will need to make your own patches, which will not, obviously, have this facility. As all good bookbinders know, it is possible to plane leather down from the suede side until it is so thin

you can almost read through it. Some do this by scraping with a convex knife blade, some with a sharp spokeshave or modelling knife, some with a low-angle block plane. Spokeshaves and planes should have the cutter honed to a slight curve, and the mouth set fairly wide, to achieve the best results.

Leather-topped desk repairs

Faced with the prospect of having to replace the leather facing of a desk top, first decide whether or not you can really afford to use leather. A desk top panel is usually quite large, so that the supplier will probably have to charge you for the whole hide, not just a portion.

Consider, instead, a plastic imitation which has much to recommend it for this purpose. It is tough, easy to keep clean, needs no feeding, comes in a great variety of colours and patterns and will not rot. Extreme cold is perhaps its worst enemy, but a desk is not likely to encounter that.

Truly old but inexpensive desks will have simply had the original leather

fixed to the top like a postage stamp with strips of veneer placed around the edges to finish off. This type is the easiest to renovate. You just scrape away the old covering scraps, thoroughly clean the bottom of the shallow tray beneath the covering, refinish the veneer and put in the new covering.

Paper templates are useful for determining the exact shape of the new panel. Once cut, it should be fitted dry, since the edges must meet the veneer accurately. If you attempt this with adhesive about, you will find that the edges are very hard to snip cleanly. A contact adhesive with a bit of slip, such as the thixotropic Dunlop Thixofix, can be used for this job. You may find, however, that you have more opportunity for adjustment if you use a PVA woodwork adhesive, spread over the top with a brush. Then you can unroll and position the vinyl covering and set the glue by means of a cool iron.

Any glue squeezed out at the edges should be wiped away with a damp rag immediately, before it sets.

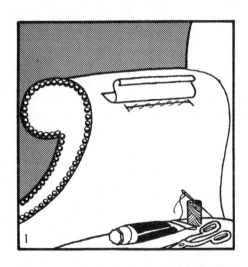

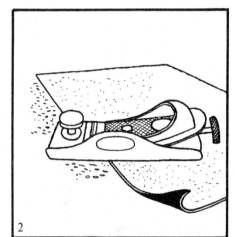

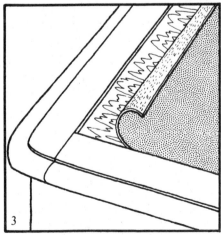

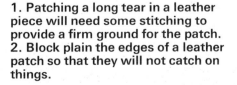

1. Patching a long tear in a leather piece will need some stitching to provide a firm ground for the patch.
2. Block plain the edges of a leather patch so that they will not catch on things.

3. On a desk top, roll out the vinyl covering over a PVA woodwork adhesive.
4. Position the covering and set the glue by pressing down with a very cool iron.

WISE BUYS

Older secondhand office furniture and ancillary equipment represent some of the best value for money in terms of residual life and sheer utility. Three main sources of supply are open to you: dealers, auctions and the private sales advertised in newspapers.

Sources of secondhand office furniture
Dealers in used office furniture may be specialists in secondhand items or they may be in business chiefly as office furnishers, who must take in items as part exchange for any new equipment which they sell. If the latter is the case, they are likely to be satisfied with lower prices than the specialists, since they make their main profit on selling new items.

Many auction sales are arranged by a legal official in charge of bankruptcy proceedings. This official arranges to sell off a business's assets to pay the debts. Much of this furniture is sold long before it has had the normal amount of wear, so it is particularly good value.

Sales of used office furniture advertised primarily through newspapers are also likely to concern little-used items. If, however, the advertiser is also the firm which has been using the furniture, the quality is probably reflected in the price.

Doorstep sales
If you work in an office you may have the chance, when any of the furniture is traded in for new, to buy the occasional piece at an exceptionally favourable price. Usually the dealer or supplier will make a list of the trade-ins, noting what he is allowing the firm against each one. Since it makes no difference to him or to the firm who actually buys any of the items, it is often possible to get what you want at the notional figure — the only difficulty being that you may have to remove it at your own expense at very short notice.

The spoils of vigilance
The bigger the collection of office furniture you can find to search among, the more numerous and pleasant your trophies can be. Force your imagination beyond the hat-stands or waste-paper baskets, even beyond tables and chairs. Take your chances with different, often overlooked items and you may find some exciting bargains.

What you may find
Although the great majority of furniture available falls into the table and chair category, an enormous variety of equipment can be the reward of a more persistent search. Trolleys with shelves are not uncommon, and you will find cabinets for books, files or drawings. The latter are very useful, having wide and shallow drawers.

Working wonders with wood
Ancient wooden pieces will most likely be sturdily built from solid wood (usually oak), internally filthy, externally battered and drearily finished. If, however, the timber is solid and relatively unwarped, you have a real find, appearances being deceptive. A good clean, complete strip and refinish will soon transform the surface, especially if you go to a little trouble to find some handsome hardware like ornamental handles.

Wooden tops and shelves can be re-faced with plastic laminate if they are too badly damaged for renovation, or if you want to use them for heat-resistant purposes.

Metamorphosis in metal
Apparently unprepossessing metal furniture may very well be worth a second look. Try to see it free from the ugly cloak of its drab, institutional grey or green paint and think only of its utility value. Structural deterioration is not encountered nearly as often in metal constructions as it is in wooden ones. Much of the battering such pieces receive damages only the paint-work, which is easily replaced.

In fact, you can usually assume that surface defects can be repaired invisibly with no great trouble. However, you should avoid items with moving parts that have ceased to operate properly, unless, of course, you are convinced that the only thing needed to put them right is a drop of oil.

Generally office furniture is mass-produced without any thought as to how it can be mended. One very good reason for this is that the cost of repairs can be almost as much as that of replacing it. Hinges, for example, are probably brazed on instead of being fastened with nuts and bolts.

Dents in sheet metal are fairly easy to deal with, unless they have deformed a door or drawer so that it will not shut properly. Small dents can be knocked out against a piece of blockboard, but use a plastic-faced hammer to avoid making a further dent in the process.

Many deeper dents, scratches or holes respond to the same treatment you might give the dents in your car: glass fibre matting, resin filler and/or cellulose putty.

Repainting
A few of the items you may come across will probably have been stove-enamelled, but most will have been given a factory coating of cellulose lacquer, assisted to dry with a bit of heat. Whatever paint is left on the metal will have very good adhesion, and will be thin enough to allow bare patches to be covered without the edges showing through.

Steel wool soap pads are effective to use in cleaning and smoothing the surface for repainting. Rinse the area well with clean water after using the pads and wipe over with methylated spirit or a mineral turpentine substitute when dry.

100 per cent polyurethane paints have the best properties for painting metal. (The 100 per cent refers to what is left on the surface when the film is dry: about 30 per cent of what you can buy consists of driers and solvents which help in the application.) If you are accustomed to using ordinary alkyd paints, which respond to being drawn out fairly thin, you have probably developed a technique that is unhelpful when it comes to working with polyurethane paints. They do not appreciate being pulled about, so be sure to study the manufacturer's recommended technique. Load the brush reasonably well, empty it in one grand gesture, lightly spread the pool of paint as far as it will easily and quickly go, then brush off with featherlight strokes. Leaving it alone at this stage may be the hardest part, but success may depend on it so do not be tempted to dab at small patches.

If you have trouble in maintaining a wet edge, remember that you can thin down pure polyurethane paints far more than you can alkyds, without affecting their toughness. A mineral turpentine substitute or heating paraffin are safe diluents. Polyurethanes take a week to reach full hardness. It is especially important on metals to allow the whole drying period.

Stick on finishes
Fabrics, wallpapers, upholstery plastics, PVC vinyl coverings can all be used to soften the harshness of metal panels. In addition, should the resonance of perhaps a cupboard top become annoying, there are self-adhesive sound-deadening pads, such as those made by Bostik for cars, which you can fix underneath.

Opposite: Office furniture is so plentiful and usually so reasonably priced that it makes good sense to use it in the home. Metal file cabinets, or office cupboards — cleaned out, painted and lined, if necessary, can do good service as containers for clothes or linen. A small desk can be the answer to your need for a dressing table, and chairs or stools, painted cheerful shiny colours are welcome anywhere.

TIN, IRON AND MARBLE

Coffee pots, hot-water jugs and similar utensils used to be made from an alloy called Britannia metal, almost entirely tin with a small percentage of antimony. It had a very pleasing, silvery colour which lost little of its brightness with use or time. Unfortunately, if you happened to forget that it was made chiefly of tin and placed it over a gas ring to keep it warm, its very low melting point immediately became apparent!

Apart from this drawback, Britannia metal was extremely serviceable, primarily because tin resists tarnishing and most common forms of chemical attack. It is this property which has made it the natural choice for protective coatings on less resistant metals, such as steel.

Tinplate is composed of very thin sheet steel which is coated on both sides by a hot-dip process with an even thinner layer of tin. The object is to combine the strength of steel with the chemically inert, softer tin. The result works beautifully — until the tin coating is pierced, from which point onwards the steel underneath begins to rust. Sometimes this happens because the tin is accidentally knocked or scratched, sometimes because it has worn thin through dust, abrasion or other storage maltreatment. In this case many rust spots can start simultaneously, giving the appearance that the tin itself is going rusty.

De-rusting techniques
The method you use to eliminate rust on a tinplate article will depend on how you intend to finish it afterwards. Generally speaking, one of the rust-removing types of paint, which turn the rust into something else, is preferable from the permanent point of view. A wash-off, rust-eating jelly may, however, be a good idea if you intend clear-sealing, especially if the rust patches are above pinhole-size. Power wire-brushing would probably do more harm than good on such thin metal.

Painting tinplate
One popular use for tinplate used to be to make hearth plates. These were used to protect the floor immediately in front of an open-fronted cooking range from hot falling cinders. If you do find one of these and intend using it in such a situation, first find yourself a heat-resistant, non-flammable paint. Originally, the plate will probably have been vitreous-enamelled.

DIY Repairs
Sheet metalwork is a skilled trade, and one that requires a great deal of expensive equipment. Unless you have exceptional knowledge, a comprehensive tool kit and a well-equipped workshop, ambitious re-forming jobs on tinplate will be difficult to carry out successfully.

Drilling and crease-flattening should be done with a piece of flat wood held under the sheet to prevent unintentional denting. Fabricated-panel constructions are best repaired with the aid of a modern pop-riveting gun, which uses hollow rivets. Once the rivet is in place, threaded through the prepared holes, the gun draws a special nail through it which turns its edges over to hold the sheets together.

Twisted hinges on tinplate boxes are especially difficult to mend. Look carefully before you buy. Do not worry about missing keys on tin-trunk locks, though. Just be glad you have been lucky enough to find a tin trunk. If you can remove the lock easily, take it to a locksmith, who can then make a new key. If you cannot get it off, try taking the whole trunk to the locksmith.

Decorating tinplate
Tinplate was often black japanned, but unless you particularly want to do a purist's renovation job, a modern 100 per cent polyurethane finish has perhaps the best combination of hardness and flexibility to cope with tinplate's tendency to flex and crease.

Self-adhesive vinyl materials can be used to good effect on tin, both internally and externally. Some felt-like nylon flock variations now on the market are especially useful for sticking to the bottoms of boxes or trays to protect table tops from scratches. The material is cut, peeled from its backing and fixed in exactly the same way as ordinary vinyl coverings, such as Fablon. Such materials could also be used to line tinplate carry-alls, dispatch-boxes and cash-boxes.

Iron age furniture and fittings
Of the many different forms which iron appears in, the two most common in the furnishing field are cast iron and wrought iron.

As a rule, an object made of cast iron indicates that the material has been cast straight from a little blast-furnace called a cupola. Hardly any measures are taken to remove impurities in the process. The iron resulting is rather coarse, needing to be cast into fairly massive forms to ensure adequate strength.

Park benches, manhole covers, garden seats and tables, street lamps and fireplaces all bear testimony to the lack of tensile strength in the metal.

Sheer mass can, however, be an advantage from the point of view of withstanding the ravages of time. Cast iron may rust, but there is plenty of it for the rust to nibble at, and even quite badly rusted pieces are well worth salvaging.

Really thick rust is unlikely to be found on fireplaces. But if you embark on de-rusting a heavily encrusted garden seat or table which constantly lives with its feet in moist ground, remember that rust can creep under any paint or lacquer you care to put on, once it is given a start. Try every means in your power to lay the object on its back so that you can get the rust off the feet. Remove rust as you would from tinplate; the only difference being that power wire-brushing may be used, especially on heavily encrusted surfaces.

Wrought iron
Any wrought iron work you find outside expensive salesrooms is more than likely done in mild steel, since the word 'wrought' now refers to the method involved in making the metal and not the metal itself.

Manufacturing wrought iron is an ancient and honourable trade, the process for refining it having been brought to perfection in the 1780s. It is an elastic metal, with a stringy, tough structure. Once it had been through the refining process it was removed from the furnaces in great blobs wound on to the ends of poles. In the process the metal never reached the molten state, so the iron already had a well-defined texture when it reached the rolling mills. By the time they had pummelled it into bars, it was the most ductile ferrous metal on the market. It was widely used wherever good nature and strength were needed — until mild steel replaced it.

Mild steel has been around for a considerable time, so if you do come across genuine wrought iron you will have quite a find. File some and see. Wrought iron files easily, but blocks the file very quickly, making it unusable after a few strokes. Neither mild steel nor cast iron have so severe an effect.

De-rusting and painting techniques are the same as those for cast iron. Much wrought iron work, however, has angles where strips are riveted or brazed together and where rust can linger if you do not take extra trouble to reach it with whatever chemical you have decided to use.

Re-using marble slabs
In the days before plastic laminates, marble was widely used for table tops — especially those used for preparing food. It was, nevertheless, always relatively expensive and appeared mainly on large scale furniture appropriate to the spacious dwellings of those people who could afford it.

A good, thick, marble top will outlast several table underframes, so you may be lucky enough to find a slab reasonably priced, in terms of cash per square metre. However, if it is very large you may have the problem of fitting it into a small place. Because it looks like hard, coloured glass, marble does tend to give the impression of being totally unyielding and indivisible, but in fact it is not very difficult to cut.

Like glass, marble is crystalline in structure, but there the similarity ends. It is far softer. A masonry-cutting disc mounted in the circular saw attachment of a handyman's power drill will cut through it, but not much faster than you could do by hand.

First of all, the slab must be scored and broken in much the same way as you would a ceramic tile, but there are important differences. Draw a clear line with a soft pencil where the

division is to be, and then continue it round all four faces: top, bottom and both front and back edges. Notch the two edges deeply with a hacksaw. You need go in only to the depth of the blade, which will be worn out by the time you finish the second notch.

Score deeply along the line on both sides, with a carbide-tipped tile-cutting tool. Then support the slab on either side of the line (a fair distance from it) and stand on it. It should only be a few inches from ground level. The result should be a clean break.

Polishing the raw edges is done with a grinding brick, a milled file or a special type of toothed plane, such as Surform, with the 508 pattern heavy-duty blade in it. To finish off, rub down with wet-and-dry abrasive paper used wet, in combination with any fine cutting compounds or polishing rouge. Remember not to leave sharp corners.

Top: Wrought or cast iron furniture need not be confined to a garden. This spacious-looking dining room has a light, out-door atmosphere which has been enhanced by using white cast iron chairs, plant stands and a cathedral stove for the main furnishings. The stove could be fitted with a light if it's no longer used for heating. Your local garage may be willing to sandblast items which are encrusted with paint and rust.
Above left: Tin fish moulds keep their shiny glow with a coat of clear polyurethane finish.
Above right: Marble slabs were once used widely for table tops and washstands but today they're a bit more unusual. It's one way of giving an ordinary chest or table a special look.

RESTORING THE GLOW TO BRASS AND COPPER

Too plentiful to be classed as a precious metal, copper has always had a high place in mankind's esteem because of its many useful properties. Perhaps more than any other metal, it is used widely in practically pure form. At its purest, it is almost as good as silver as a conductor of heat and electricity.

Pleasant in colour and easy to handle, copper is highly resistant to weather and salt water corrosion. It will, however, over a long period of time, form a green 'rust' on its surface. This coating can be quite attractive on some things, such as building domes, and the initial thin layer seems to protect the underlying metal. Household items that you may come across made from relatively pure copper will be those which require good heat conductivity such as kettles, saucepans, frying pans and warming pans.

A sociable metal
Copper very readily forms alloys with other metals, but in the secondhand field the two most frequently encountered are brass and bronze.

The brass group
Copper + zinc = brass is a very simple equation for this metal. Generally, alloys containing more than 80 per cent copper are used as gilding metals. Their richer colouring makes them especially useful for making things like costume jewellery. The ordinary articles you might encounter, such as paraffin lamps, doorknobs and candlesticks, are more likely to be made in Muntz metal — roughly 60 per cent copper to 40 per cent zinc.

The bronzes
Copper and tin alloyed together make bronze. You are most likely to encounter gunmetal bronzes, which have a bit less copper in them than coinage-alloy types, a little more tin and odd scraps of zinc, lead and/or nickel.

Spit and polish
Neither brass nor bronze is liable to quite such severe discoloration as neglected copper. Normally it responds very well to ordinary metal polishes. These usually consist of a weak acid and a selection of abrasives, perhaps with a little wax to help the shine along.

Copper cooking utensils may give you some cleaning problems, due to contact with heat and fumes. Those in the picture, for example, were almost totally black when they were bought. Vinegar with plenty of salt boiled up in it was used to clean them, helped by a bit of scouring powder. The mixture was rubbed onto the pots with a nylon scouring pad until brightness returned to the metal. As soon as this stage was reached, the pans were rinsed and dried. Had they been left wet, the dark copper oxide would have formed again.

Mending leaks
Holes in copper or brass utensils may be the result of general wear, particularly if an item has been used for cooking and so been subjected to repeated scouring. If the metal has worn paper-thin, its cooking days are over, but it may still have a decorative role to play. In this event, you need only disguise the hole by filling it up with car-body resin filler. This can then be dabbed with metallic copper-coloured lacquer, such as that made by Rustins.

Repairs for active service
If a hole has been accidentally made in still serviceably thick and sound metal, or if a metal seam is leaking, such as around a kettle's spout, or along a seam in a paraffin lamp's reservoir, a soldered repair is the best and most permanent solution.

Solder is produced by amalgamating lead with tin or other metals to make a compound which will melt easily, flow into any cranny and bond instantly to the metal. By altering the proportions of the different ingredients, the solder's melting point can be predetermined. You can always find a grade which will melt before your copper or brass utensil does (very important) but which will not melt again at cooking temperatures (equally important). It helps if you can explain

Left: A collection of copper pots makes a handsome surround for a kitchen fireplace — or can look equally well hanging against a wall.
Above: The rich look of brass is used for all sorts of easy-to-find household items — from bed frames and lamps to door knobs. Don't be put off if some old brass pieces are coated with a brown, shoe-polish like substance: a hard scrub with a metal polish should restore their looks.

what you want to use the solder for when you buy it.

Solder will not bond firmly unless the metal is completely free from oxides, a condition difficult to obtain, since oxidation is speeded up when a metal is heated. Strips of solder with a core of flux will solve this problem. The flux either seals the metal off from the air to stop oxides from forming or it removes the oxides chemically, according to whether it is an active or a passive kind of flux.

Chemical colour changing
Corroded brass or copper might look uncomfortably brash and new after the scouring you have been obliged to give for cleaning. Provided that you have a decently polished surface on the metal, you can treat it with chemicals to alter its colour to some degree. You must always take the obvious precautions against skin or eye contact and against spillage, but the results

can be well worth a little extra trouble.

One of the simplest mixtures to use is a weak solution of ammonium sulphide. A good soaking in this will give brass a golden hue, or copper a reddish one. The strength of the solution can be varied quite a bit — a stronger solution and/or longer soaking will produce various shades of black, brown, red or yellow. Always rinse the metal after using this solution, and finish off with a coat of lacquer. Polyurethane or melamine clear lacquers are probably the most suitable for decorative purposes.

Antiquing brass and copper
To give brass a green/brown colour, make up a solution of copper nitrate in water by adding 100 grammes of copper nitrate to 100 millilitres of water, with larger or smaller amounts pro rata. Do not add the water to the chemical. (This is a good general rule

to follow when dealing with all chemicals: the reason being that the heat generated could vaporize water droplets which could then spit in your eye.) Heat the solution to a temperature of 60°C (140°F) and brush it all over the metal every few hours throughout a day. Leave the article overnight.

Dry it off by placing the item in a warm oven for a little while, then rub French chalk over it with a soft brush. Finally remove any traces of the chalk with a dry rag, and lacquer over.

It is possible to 'silver' brass, for a clock face, perhaps. To do this use a paste consisting of 10 grammes of silver chloride, 20 grammes of cream of tartar and 30 grammes of common salt. Grind all the ingredients up and mix with just enough water to make it into a paste the consistency of cream. Rub the paste over the brass with a soft rag until you have the degree of silvering you want, then wash off the excess, dry and lacquer.

SILVER AND CHROME

Chromium is an extremely hard metal, and a rather expensive one, so solid chromium items are virtually non-existent. It appears mainly as a thin, electro-plated film on literally thousands of common, everyday things made from cheaper materials.

The character of chromium
Most of the problems with chromium plating arise when it is applied to iron or steel. Although hard, the film of chromium is porous, allowing moisture through to whatever is immediately beneath it. Good chromium plating consists of a thin coat of copper to give good adhesion to the basic metal, a fat layer of nickel (which is non-porous) over this and a final film of chromium.

Items such as bathroom fittings are usually made of brass, and receive a specially heavy coat of nickel, but those made of iron or steel do not, and should be watched carefully for signs of rust. Minute black pits are the first hint that water has penetrated to corrodible metal. Leave the pitted chrome untreated and the rust will creep along the ferrous metal's surface to undermine the plating completely, so that it just flakes away.

Protecting sound chrome
Unpitted plating can be protected quite adequately by frequent applications of one of the heavier wax polishes which have been specially made for the chrome parts of motor vehicles. Make certain, however, that the polish claims to seal out moisture for lengthy periods, not just to clean.

Treating pitted chrome
Waxes will only succeed if you seal off the pores in the chromium before any moisture has penetrated to start rust spots. Once pitted, you must deal with the rust, however minute in quantity. Any proprietary rust remover will do some good, but for this particular problem you should choose one, such as Kurust, that does not have to be washed off with water. These change the rust chemically into a non-corroding compound and are the most likely to work.

These rust removers are especially effective in stopping rust under chrome, but often introduce other problems. Some varieties refuse to dry soundly over the good plating. When this happens, the chrome will neither shine nor support lacquer properly, unless you follow up with a specially made companion wash to remove the surplus, chemically-unchanged compound. Once this has been done, a glossy, transparent polyurethane lacquer will seal off the treated surface completely, long-lastingly and almost invisibly.

Badly rusted plating
Provided that there is no extensive flaking or lifting of the plating film, even quite severely rusted chrome plate can be rescued for a time if you precede the remover/wash/lacquer treatment with a steel wool scrub. Domestic soap pads will do, if you rinse well enough and dry off all the water before you put the remover on. The lacquer will effectively disguise much of the unavoidable fine scratching made by the steel wool. Maintenance should not involve more than the occasional clean, (not polish), and new application of lacquer.

Chromium-plated plastic
Rust cannot upset plating on plastic surfaces, of course. However, because plastics are electrically non-conductive, the metal plating relies on electro-static attraction for its bond. This remains strong unless the thin plating is punctured. If that happens, it will very soon peel off entirely. There is no

Opposite: Chrome is a good metal to use in combination with ultra-modern and older furniture styles. Here, a stylish breakfast nook is composed of traditional wooden dining room chairs, a chrome and glass table and a half-globe, hanging chrome lampshade. The simple lines are complemented by the black and white colour scheme.
Right: Many quaint items are made of silver or silver plate – from ornate photograph frames and unusual tableware to clocks and hip flasks! Pewter things are usually large and simple, like coffee pots or mugs.

known cure for this, short of replating, and it is not worth replating cheap plastic objects.

Replating

Replating is not just a question of flashing an isolated patch with a new metal surface. It involves stripping the old plating completely, usually by shotblasting, repolishing the stripped surface and putting on all three plating layers afresh – to a standard appropriate to the intended use of the article. Much of the cost is accounted for by the work involved in obtaining a new, bare, highly polished, original metal base for the electro-plating process. You can, therefore, expect it to rise steeply with the object's size and weight.

Silver of sorts

Pure silver is very rarely met with, partly because it is expensive and partly because it is very soft and pliable. It is normally alloyed with baser metals such as copper and zinc, making a stronger, more hardwearing metal. The proportion of silver in these alloys is given in terms of parts of silver per 1,000 of the alloy. This proportion is known as 'fineness'. Sterling silver has a fineness of 925 – it contains 92·5 per cent silver and 7·5 per cent other metal.

Whatever the quality of the workmanship, solid silver articles now command high prices on the secondhand market, simply as sources of a scarce material. Things made of a silver alloy are slightly more common, but still relatively expensive. Indeed, few secondhand items are likely to consist of silver alloy throughout, but will be silver plated instead.

Silver plate

Most common and reasonably priced silver goods will have been electroplated after they were made. Signs of copper showing through worn patches indicate that a thing is plated, as do the stamped letters: EPNS (Electro-Plated Nickel Silver, an alloy of copper, zinc and nickel). Spoons and forks are almost invariably plated with this

silver-coloured metal because it is hardwearing.

Removing tarnish

Left to itself, silver eventually turns black because of the film of silver sulphide which forms on it. Whether you use a slightly abrasive special cleaner or one of the dip-in solvents, you inevitably remove a thin layer of the silver every time you polish. Do it only when you have to, and then only sparingly. Chased lines should not be scraped clean: they are supposed to retain some tarnish. Very intricately chased pieces should be cleaned with one of the polishes which is easy to get out of the crevices and will not leave a thick deposit of white cream. If there are heavy, noticeable deposits already embedded in the crevices, a

stiff scrub with an old toothbrush before cleaning will remove the worst.

Pewter pots

Other things are made from pewter, of course, but pots or dishes are the most common items made from this alloy of lead and tin (and occasionally other materials). These items are always solid pewter, which is cleaned just like brass, copper or zinc. If your chosen polish instructs you to buff the metal to a shine before the polish is quite dry, there may well be a waxy residue left on the surface. This should be washed off thoroughly before drinking or eating out of a pewter utensil. Otherwise, there is little to worry about, so long as you do not put a pewter item on a hotplate, provoking it to melt.

FIRST AID FOR CHINA

Judging from the contents of the average antique shop, old pottery, earthenware, and porcelain china must be the most plentiful relics of bygone ages in existence. The sheer fragility of the finer items, however, must mean that their ranks are steadily reducing in numbers and that you are unlikely to be able to replace a damaged piece with a similar one if it was made some time ago.

In any case, whether you originally bought it or whether you inherited it, your pretty or useful treasure (perhaps both) probably has a sentimental value for you out of all proportion to its monetary value. The vast majority of rare pieces will long since have been tracked down and had their whereabouts charted by both professional and amateur hunters. If you smash or chip anything in this category, its repair is probably best left to the experts, who use skilled and specialized methods, like re-firing.

In the case of less pretentious pottery, there is quite a bit you can do at home, by simple methods, towards helping it back to a useful if not too active life.

Adhesives

Glues and cements formulated to stick broken edges of ceramic ware together were once made from shellac. Perhaps more successful were the hard-setting cement type, but no adhesives now on the market are stronger than those based on epoxy resin. These were originally developed for airframe construction, and have as good a grip on glass and smooth metal as they have on more porous substances.

Most of these glues have one grave disadvantage: they take an inordinately long time to set at normal room temperatures, some as long as three days. It is possible, however, to reduce the setting time to hours if the join can be subjected to moderate heat, say in a cool oven. When this is not practicable, use a variety of quick setting epoxy adhesive, such as that made by Borden. These have become available only comparatively recently, so you may have to search a little to find one.

Surface chips

Chips which are really craters in the surface, rather than pieces broken bodily from an edge, are easily filled with one of the many modelling compounds used by sculptors and industrial designers. Stickier and trickier to use is an epoxy adhesive with powder colours mixed in. Obviously you will not have to bother with the pigmentation if you are going to paint any design features back in after gluing. This is only of value when the design of the piece is relatively simple.

Edge chips

Epoxy adhesive is equally suitable to use for repairing damaged edges. It will fill the space very firmly once set, but since there is nothing to support it until it has set you will have a delicate application problem — not an insuperable one, just awkward. One way of providing temporary backing is to press a flat wad of putty or plasticine on to the surrounding sound surface, to give the adhesive a depression to fill, instead of a yawning gap. Both putty and plasticine contain quite a bit of oil, so should not give any trouble when you want to remove them.

Clean breaks

Fresh fractures involving no splintering or crumbling away are the simplest of all to mend, and the most likely to remain hidden when repaired. Adhesives for china and for pottery are generally colourless or white, and have always been so. Anything that shows up on a mended article as a dark line is not glue, but dirt.

Dirty edges

Dark line trouble occurs as a rule when a piece breaks along a previously mended join, or is left for a lengthy period between being broken and being repaired.

Previously glued breakages will give the greatest difficulty, because their edges will not allow a fresh adhesive toe-hold until all the old glue is off — and it just may have been an epoxy. Luckily, this is not very probable. However, if you try immersing the piece in near-boiling water (do not simmer it), acetone, ammonia, or methylated spirit and it proves immune to each in turn (not all at once), suspect the worst and abandon the attempt. Remember to wash off one solvent before you try the next, so that each gets a fair chance.

Once you have removed the old glue, a strongish solution of household detergent in hot water, with a small amount of domestic bleach dissolved in it (about an egg-cupful to the gallon) should leave clean edges. Deeply ingrained soiling will only come out after a prolonged soak. On exceptionally stubborn items, it is better to leave them submerged in the solution for weeks, rather than increase the strength of the bleach. Strong bleaches may leave crystal deposits in the porous clay, which would be difficult to get out and which might upset the adhesive.

Rinse thoroughly and dry off the clean edges before re-gluing.

Mending methods

Apply the adhesive sparingly; too much will not make for a neat join because the excess in between the mating edges would tend to keep them apart. In addition, once this excess is squeezed out it makes it difficult to see whether or not the pieces are cramped together properly.

Sticky tape of some kind will probably be the only feasible means of holding the parts close together for the requisite length of time, even five or six minutes being a bit of an ordeal by hand pressure alone. Cellulose clear tape will work well for short stints, but when you have to cramp something together for three days its adhesive may dry and its grip loosen a little. Professional repairers normally use a brown-paper tape (common office type). If you use this, bear in mind that it shrinks as it dries out: a very helpful property, provided there is tape on both sides of the join.

Cracked but not broken

Professional pottery restorers and others of stout heart can sometimes mend cracks running from the body of a piece to one edge without deliberately completing the fracture. If you feel you have nothing to lose, try pulling the crack a little wider to see if the trick is possible. Provided that it will open sufficiently to allow a bit of card, or anything stiff and thin, to be inserted to hold it open, adhesive can be worked stingily into it with a fine brush. Then release the wedge and tape the join.

Should you pull a bit too hard when springing the crack open, you will either be lucky and simply complete the break or you will be unlucky and produce further fractures. Attempting crack-springing repairs is never a sure thing. Always try to protect your hands when doing such work.

Putting the pattern back

However well a crack is mended, gaps may remain in the pattern or picture that are just too blatant to be ignored. Artist's acrylic or oil colours are both quite satisfactory to use over the adhesive, although the matching-in will be mainly a matter of trial and error. In any event it is worth the attempt since errors can easily be rubbed out with a rag dipped in the appropriate solvent for the paint you are using.

A clear lacquer is needed to replace the lost glaze, or at least the appearance of it. In the absence of one made specifically for the purpose, an acid-catalyzed lacquer will make an adequate substitute. It is both water-clear and heat-resistant, although the latter virtue is unimportant if you only intend to display the piece.

Enamelware

True enamel consists of glass, in the form of coloured powder, which has been fused on to the surface beneath it by the application of heat. When enamel is chipped, it presents one of the most difficult repair problems. No paint can imitate its effect properly and refiring to add new enamel is out of the question because the old enamel could not withstand the necessary heat.

The only substance which can be applied cold and which will set to anything approaching an enamel surface is a liquid plastic sold mainly in kits for hobbyists, such as that made by Enamelcraft. It acquires its gloss as it flows to find its own level. To make it stable on an uneven surface, you must let it partially set first.

Being a plastic, the 'paint' can embody powder colour, but not necessarily with predictable results. It does, however, offer an interesting way of transforming dull earthenware that is not enamelled to begin with.

Right above: Do not be hasty and discard a favourite plate or pretty jug if it becomes cracked or chipped. With patience most repairs can be made without leaving noticeable scars. **Right below:** Broken handles on cups and mugs are one of the most frequent mishaps with china. They are easy to mend if the break is a clean one. Make sure no glue or grease remain round the break, and use an epoxy resin adhesive for the repair. To support a simple break while the adhesive sets use clear sticky tape, fixed crosswise and lengthwise around the handle. If it is broken in two places, try supporting it with plasticine as well. Broken plates can be supported underneath with an identically shaped plate greased so it can be easily removed when the adhesive dries.

MIRROR AND GLASS TO REFLECT UPON

Glass is a crystalline material. When it is clean and new this is not too apparent, but with advancing age and consequent exposure to the ravages of the environment it gradually becomes more brittle and more obviously crystalline.

This, however, is only one reason that glass loses its clarity. Another is that the surface (which is actually slightly porous) tarnishes and darkens when it comes under attack from chemicals in the atmosphere, smoke, light, running water and contact with other materials.

Kinds of glass
Molten glass may be formed into solid lumps by pouring into very simple moulds, cast into more intricate shapes in complex moulds, drawn into rods or tubes, rolled into thin sheets or blown into hollow forms, with or without the assistance of moulds. Additives can colour it, harden, soften or toughen it.

It is almost always possible to judge the delicacy of a glass item just from its appearance.

In the secondhand field, most of the inexpensive glassware you find will be fairly thick-walled blown glass, or heavy plate glass, in mirrors, for example.

Repairs to glass
Cracks, breaks, chips and scratches are more difficult to deal with in glass than in a material like china because glass is so hard all the way through. Besides this, to be successful the repair must not affect its translucence.

For this reason, surface chips are most difficult to fill invisibly. Luckily, the only fault in aged glass which is impossible to repair is a deep scratch. Almost every other trouble is capable of at least a partial solution.

Cracks
Cracks can be mended with an epoxy resin adhesive in much the same way as porcelain and the other ceramics, but it is always a wise precaution to clean the mating edges very thoroughly with methylated spirit before applying the adhesive. This is done to eliminate any trace of grease or oil, both arch-enemies of good adhesion, especially where epoxy and metal or glass are concerned.

Since most sticky tapes will not adhere well to a glass surface, give the same treatment to any surfaces which you must support with tapes. It should improve the adhesion.

Filling chips
If you want to attempt filling chips in glass, try a liquid plastic of the type sold for embedding things. It comes in a clear form but will take colours. Exact matching may present problems. The hobby varieties, such as Plasticraft, are very powerful adhesives, so will stay put without difficulty if you let the hardener begin its action before application.

Although it is possible to handle the hardened plastic after twenty-four hours, ideally it needs a week to

cure before it sets to its fullest extent.

Liquid plastic will come off your hands easily enough if you allow it to dry crisp and then rub hard. Removing it from anything else is like trying to get a limpet off a rock at low tide.

If you do not particularly want to tackle chip filling yourself, you can have them ground out professionally, at your own risk. The cost will probably be quite high because it is a skilled and time-consuming job.

Discoloration
When glass has tarnished or darkened, consider whether the patina really needs to be removed. You may want to retain an antique look about the article for some reason. If you do decide that the discoloration is nothing but an

46

ugly nuisance, you must take off the soiled top layer of glass, to reach the clean, untarnished glass underneath it. Chemicals such as ammonia may dissolve staining, but the eroded glass surface they produce will not be dissolved with it. There is no safe way for the average person to dissolve glass.

Fine abrasives are the best home solution for an eroded glass surface. Try metal polish, toothpaste, jeweller's rouge, or car-body rubbing compounds, but not scouring powders.

Mirrors

Most of the mirrors on old furniture will be tarnished in front and de-silvered behind, good for neither use nor ornament. Unless there is some decorative feature on the face, or the whole mirror has an elaborate and unreproducible form, it will most probably be both economical and practical to buy a new mirror, rather than go to the trouble and expense of having an old one resilvered.

If you do decide to have a mirror reconditioned and it is to be fixed in place with screws, have any necessary screw holes drilled through it at the same time. It is not difficult to drill holes through the glass yourself, but in the case of a mirror you run the risk of removing part of the silvering in the process.

Drilling holes in glass

For drilling holes in glass, a firm, dispensable base to lay the glass on, or a specially designed (by you) support for a bottle or other unstable form, a hand drill and a spear-pointed or triangular-tipped drill are the basic essentials. If you can arrange to have a water tap running gently on the drill as you work, so much the better. If you are drilling an old mirror, omit the water lubricant in case it should damage the silvering. The special drill has a tungsten carbide tip, only a little bit softer than a diamond, so there is no need to exert overmuch pressure or to turn the handle fast and furiously.

Work carefully and steadily. Rinse the glass dust away if you can. If you cannot, at least flush the hole out with a little water (or methylated spirit if it's an old mirror) and mop up the drillings with a wad of wet cotton wool.

Cleaning untarnished glass

Methylated spirit is quick and effective to use for cleaning glass, but

absolutely taboo where you have French polished wood around the panes – as you might on a display cabinet. Liquid metal polishes may also attack French polish, but try them first on small, inconspicuous areas. You may be lucky. Do not use any non-transparent cleaner on frosted or non-reflective glass or you may leave traces. Matt picture glass is quite fragile so always handle it carefully.

Jars and globes with découpage

Glass containers of most shapes and sizes can be decorated in a personal and fascinating way by using the art of découpage. To achieve this effect, the glass object must have a hole through which you can position cut-out pictures. Almost any kind of picture or pattern is suitable, so long as its visible surface will take a clear adhesive.

Once you have spread the glue thinly over the picture surface, use bits of stick, bent wire or anything else which will enable you to position the pictures inside the container. The task can be frustrating, but the final result is well worth the painstaking effort.

To complete the process, pour emulsion paint into the jar or globes, swill it around until it covers all the unpictured glass, then pour it out. Inevitably a bit of paint will dribble between picture and glass here and there, but if you have fixed the pictures securely to the glass, this should not be enough to mar the final effect.

FRAME-UP

Left to themselves, picture frames will perform their function with little trouble. Old age catches up on them in the fullness of time, causing the wood to shrink and the glue to lose its grip, but it is rare for one to give way suddenly and unload its contents on to the floor.

Picture frame repairs

If you go hunting for secondhand frames to buy at bargain prices, however, you are bound to find an abundance of unloved and ill-treated ones. Naturally a hard life can loosen the corner joints of the stoutest frame. In general you should find that the bigger frames last better than the smaller ones, as they would have been made to support heavy loads of glass and canvas.

Where there is no splitting or breaking away of the wood, corner joints can often be held together with another nail or two and a little fresh glue, possibly without taking any of the other joints apart. The glue would have to be hot-melt, woodworking adhesive, such as Scotch glue — more modern ones having no affinity for that already in the wood.

It's also asking for trouble to use bigger nails than the originals. If you are convinced that there is not enough sound wood to hold small ones, it is far better to drill pilot holes and substitute a fairly long brass screw. If you adopt this method, sink the screw deeply enough below the wood surface to allow for filling later.

Tightening old joints

Slighter, smaller frames are usually held together by simple, mitred joints, the members being butted together, pinned and glued. Better-class frames, in the larger sizes at least, have proper fitted joints — open mortice and tenon, or halved — modified to incorporate the necessary mitres.

These joints tend to loosen when the wood has dried out through age or modern heating, or when the glue has decayed. One effective cure for this is to take the whole frame apart, clean up all the joint surfaces and cramp them together again, repacked with a PVA wood glue and scraps of thin veneer to compensate for the shrinkage.

It is possible to buy frame cramps quite cheaply, made from plastic and nylon or terylene cord. They are quite simple to make as well, consisting simply of four L-shaped pieces of wood held tightly in to the corners of the frame by a strong cord running all the

way around. Notches in the corner apexes stop the cord from slipping off. It can then be tightened with a short length of wood which acts as a tourniquet.

Provided that the inside angle of each corner-block is a true 90°, the frame will be pulled into a decent rectangle in this way. You can pin the joints instead, but it is more difficult to keep them square. Nevertheless, you may have to use very small nails or panel pins if the frame is ornate.

Cutting a frame to size

To reduce the size of a large frame simply measure the size of the picture to go in it, unfasten two diagonally opposite corners and cut all four sides down to the appropriate size. You will probably need to use a mitre box to get accurate angles. Re-glue the corners and clamp firmly until dry. Use a try-square to see that each corner is a right angle.

Patching up the decoration

Sometimes only a very small portion has been knocked out of the superimposed moulding and sculpture on a frame. If you think you can bridge the gap with a reasonably accurate imitation of the design, fill it in with a cellulose or resin filler and carve in the missing detail when it has set hard.

Long stretches are better if replaced entirely with modern plastic moulding, which may have to be substituted for the original decoration on all sides.

Frame finishes

It may very well be that you liked the look of your ornate frame before you patched it up, and do not want it to look brash and new. Be that as it may, the fillings and patches must be painted if they are not to stick out like sore thumbs. The best way of blending them in is to repaint the entire frame the same colour. Using a darker shade of gold paint, or dulling it down with a little bronze colour from the same range might help to soften the effect, but if that is insufficient you may have to fall back on deliberate aging techniques.

Gentle scrubbing of dirt into the crevices of the moulding with a soft brush is quite effective. Exposure to bright sunlight is also a good method, although it takes time and cannot be done with the picture in situ. Dullness without dirtiness may be enough to take off the rawness of new colour. Matt, rather dark tinted varnish painted on top of the gold could accomplish this much.

Plain wooden frames which have had new wood inserted respond well to dust rubbed on with a dark-coloured wax polish. Remember, the disguise does not need to be total, so long as you can remove the sharpness from the dividing line between the new and the old.

New wood can be given a soft patina in a very short time, by purposeful rubbing with a scrap piece of smooth hardwood, preferably harder than the wood it is treating.

Reglazing a frame

Fitting a new piece of non-reflective glass in a frame makes sound sense, even if the existing glass is still unbroken, because the fine surface etching eliminates all specular reflection and allows the picture to be seen clearly from virtually any angle.

Non-reflective glass needs two sorts of special care: handle it gently because it is rather thin; and remember where you put it down because it has no shine to make it obvious and you could easily lean your hand on it by mistake. Fragility makes it inadvisable to trim edges to fit, so measure accurately, allowing up to an extra millimetre all around for clearance.

The glass goes into the frame rebate first (underside of the frame), then the mask if there is one (perhaps for a print or photograph), then the picture itself. Unless the back of the picture already comes flush with that of the frame, packing must go in so that the final covering of brown paper over the back of the picture can lie smoothly, and be fixed to the edges with brown-paper tape. Thin polyether foam makes a safe packing.

Display frames

You may come across deep frames with stiff backboards on which pretty or interesting collections of objects can be mounted for display. If they can be pinned on, like butterflies, a special hardboard is available which is made to hold pins.

Plywood backboards can be covered with fabric, or painted. Fixings must suit the displayed item, of course. Some solid items can be screwed into the board and so anchored from the back. Others may have to be sewn or tied, or fastened with adhesive.

Alternative jobs for frames

Without a picture or other content, a frame may be considered simply as a surround, defining and enhancing a plain or patterned panel. Some of your ideas for exploiting the focusing power of a frame may involve putting strains on its structure that it was never intended to withstand. If, for example, you want to use a large frame to edge a bed-head panel or to act as a surround for a glass-topped coffee table, you should make sure that the backing boards make up in rigidity what the frame may lack.

With this proviso, almost anything is possible. If a frame is to carry loads without the support of a backboard, some strengthening should be given the corners. Steel or brass L-plates screwed to the back could be the simplest reinforcement to use.

1. to 3. If you want to strengthen the corners of a frame without dismantling it, you can drill diagonally through the corner pieces and glue in wooden dowels. You might also try screwing diagonal or triangular corner plates of plywood or metal at the back of a damaged frame.

4. To refasten the corners of frames, glue and then tie them with string as shown, until the glue sets. Use a PVA woodwork adhesive for best results.

5. & 6. Small pieces of broken moulding on frames can be repaired with plastic wood. Larger pieces can be replaced by taking an impression with modelling clay from a sound section of moulding. Use cellulose filler paste to make a cast of this. Sand down rough edges and glue the new piece in place with an epoxy resin glue.

7. Wax gilts make excellent substitutes for gold leaf when regilding a frame. Simply rub the wax on with a finger or cloth; a small stiff brush should be used to reach cracks and crevices. Protect this gilt with some type of clear alcohol-based varnish.

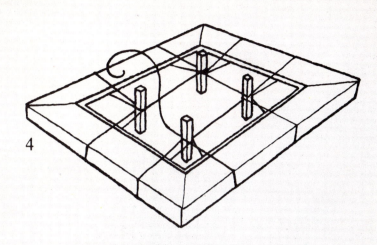

4

5

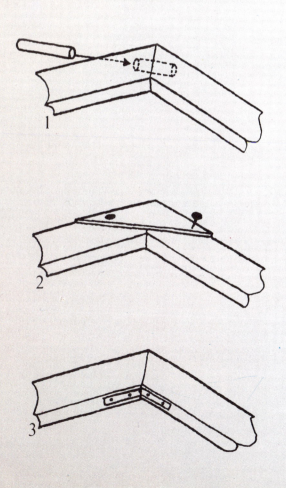

1

2

3

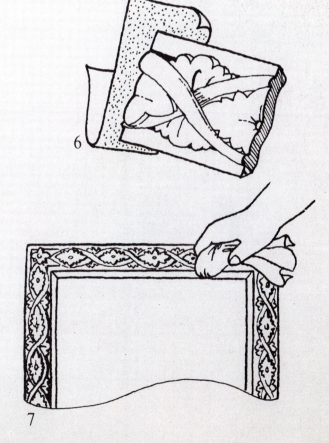

6

7

THE INSIDES OF THINGS

Has-been furniture made originally to contain things may never have been finished properly on the inside. The men who made it were not skimping or idle, but simply suiting whatever lining they used to its intended task.

Lining boxes, chests and small caskets was then and is now a trade in itself, quite separate from that of making containers. Only rarely will you be able to retain an original lining, which in any case may be badly deteriorated. Even sound linings may have been removed to allow the outside to be properly renovated. Usually, it cannot be put back, and the finish underneath it will almost certainly be unfit to take a new, sealed finish, without a great deal of preparation.

Modern materials, fortunately, offer tremendous advantages over older types — and they require little expertise in application.

Small boxes and cases
Cushioning and colour are usually the important attributes of lining materials used for small containers, rather than exceptional resistance to wear or damp. Baize, felt and padded silk were the traditional inner surfaces, and sometimes velvet or an imitation of it. Modern synthetic fabrics such as nylon, and imitations of leather in PVC vinyls, can provide hardwearing interiors if you especially need them. Padding is easily achieved with foam rubber or plastic.

Self-supporting materials such as felt and self-adhesive velours can be fixed directly on to the sides, lids and bottoms of small boxes, since you can cut them accurately to fit before having to glue them in place. For something like a cutlery case, you can make a far more professional job, and one more in keeping with its character, by using velvet material. However, you will have continual trouble with fraying edges if you simply stick it straight on to the box. The classic way is to mount each small panel separately, before putting it into place.

Cut thin, stiff, supporting pieces of cardboard for the panels, each one slightly smaller all around than its respective panel. To achieve the optimum precision, cut the pieces of card to size with a modelling knife or scalpel and steel ruler, rather than

scissors. The corresponding pieces of velvet must be cut with enough spare material to wrap neatly over the card without any overlap of velvet-on-velvet at the back. Corners are notched out of the velvet to avoid the same trouble. Glue is applied only between the back flaps of velvet and the back of the card, so there is no danger of staining the velvet where it will be seen once the panels are fixed in place. Use a flexible-bond adhesive, such as Copydex.

Adhesive should be applied over the whole back area of each panel, but sparingly, to avoid accidental oozings that might mar the finished appearance. The instructions which accompany the adhesive will probably advise coating both surfaces, allowing them to dry somewhat and then bringing them together. This procedure produces an impact adhesive, which you do not really need for this job. Instead, coat the fabric panel and press it gently into place while the adhesive is still tacky. If you do decide to use the impact adhesion method, you cannot afford to make the slightest error when positioning the panels — once the two glued surfaces touch they will bond.

If you would prefer a cushioned look — thin layers of plastic foam can be sandwiched between card and fabric. A buttoned effect is easily obtained by stitching through the fabric and foam. Obviously you will need to allow for the extra thickness of the padding when cutting the card. If you do not want a buttoned effect, stick the foam to the card, but not the fabric to the foam.

Large drawers and shelves
Linings for these shelves and drawers are rarely seen, so new ones can be chosen for their sheer practicality. PVC self-adhesive sheeting is a natural choice, but vinyl-faced wallpaper comes a close second — since it does not have to be stuck down.

To get an accurate fit with these sizeable pieces it helps first to cut a brown-paper template. Its edges can be folded and refolded to get an exact fit into angles and corners. Even self-adhesive materials, which can be cut to fit before the backing is taken off, benefit from the use of a template.

Above: Paper, felt, hessian and other fabrics make practical and good-looking linings for household containers.
Opposite: Line both the inside and the outside of furniture to imitate the surrounding decor.

Wallpaper linings
The inside surfaces of large cupboards, wardrobes and bookcases are ideal sites for relatively small amounts of exotically patterned or super-costly wallpaper which you would not usually use on walls or ceilings. Shops frequently have odd remnant rolls for sale at special low prices after stocktaking — never enough for a room, but ample for a wardrobe. Few old-fashioned wardrobes will have sheer sides or backs, so templates also help here to fit the panels precisely.

It may be difficult or inadvisable to use standard wallpaper adhesive for this application, so try a simple test on a small corner of the wood to see if the varnish or other finish reacts. If it does, filled resin emulsion types, such as Clam 143, are often a good alternative choice.

Wallpaper, especially richly coloured or textured, shows to excellent advantage on the inside backs and sides of glass-fronted bookcases or other show-cupboard pieces. The idea is far from new, but not as widely used as it should be. Remember that it will be protected from the soiling that normal wallpapers are subjected to, so constant redecoration will not be necessary.

Wallpaper patchwork
Panels are small areas to deal with compared with walls and ceilings, so it is perfectly feasible to work original arrangements of paper patchwork on them to create a striking and unique decor.

It's rather difficult to work in situ on what can be quite a fussy job. Unless the arrangement is very simple, cut out a perfectly fitting backing sheet to allow the whole design to be pre-fabricated on a flat surface.

Patchwork may at first seem a rather haphazard method of decoration but the most effective and arresting designs are anything but that. Bold and simple themes are much more likely to be successful than busy, detailed patterns. Simple geometrical designs in contrasting shades of fairly plain paper are both easy to do and striking to look at. Hexagonal patches in random groups will also stand out well.

You will find it easier to make a patchwork if you cut the pattern from a solid template, made of thin sheet metal or plastic laminate. Set the template in place over the wallpaper and using its edges as a guide, cut out the shape with a fine knife. Naturally, you should not do this on the carpet. Hardboard makes a good cutting base. Let light colours predominate in the pattern. It will be easier to see things inside, especially if the unit is itself in a dark area.

Fabrics as linings

Fabric linings can be just as effective as wallpapers, but it should not be fixed permanently to the interior of a unit unless they are paper-backed – like proprietary hessian coverings. Cleaning or replacement will eventually be necessary for all linings, and it will be easier if the material is not permanently fixed.

All the same, fabrics normally have a softer texture than papers and can make interiors look especially inviting. The fabric can be mounted on sheets of thin hardboard which are cut to fit the units. Wrap the material round the panel and fix it at the back, as for the smaller cutlery box panels. The hardboard panels are simply held in place with small brass screws and screw caps, which enable them to be removed very quickly for cleaning.

USELESS
TO USEFUL

In your searches for usable second-hand things you may well find many an item put aside long ago because the purpose for which it was created no longer exists. Either because they were solidly constructed or because they have had little use, many will still be in fine condition, ready to put in a lifetime of service for anyone with the imagination to find a use for them.

Old barrels
Beer now travels more often than not in modern metal containers, which are lighter, more hygienic and rarely need repair. Every now and again a supply of old oak barrels is disposed of in favour of the metal ones. If you are lucky enough to get hold of one of these it can be made into a serviceable and novel outdoor table.

No amount of rainwater is likely to affect oak badly, but it will retain its appearance better if you stand the barrel on a hard level base, made to drain effectively. Most barrels will collect water in the top of the lid, so either drill through the rim or notch it to allow the water to drain away. If you like the look of the wood as it is, leave it unfinished or give it a matt polyurethane varnish. If you feel it is too drab, paint it bright colours with a polyurethane finish.

Oak barrels are pretty heavy, and consequently quite stable, but if you find the top too small for the number of people who are to use it, add a false table top in exterior quality blockboard, such as the Cresta brand. This can be screwed to the barrel's lid, but remember to use bright zinc-plated screws to avoid rusting. Should the new top tend to make the barrel tip, stabilize it by filling wholly or partially with sand or stones.

Victorian mantels
Some of these elaborate structures of wood, marble, metal and glass are very gracefully proportioned and contain useful little features like shelves, drawers, hanging-hooks, mirrors, and occasionally even built-in frames for photographs. Usually well-built and quite strong they come on the market only too rarely. If you are looking for a mantel, try to salvage one from a house due for demolition.

If you are lucky enough to find such a piece, but do not have a fireplace of the right scale for it, consider turning it into a bedhead.

If its finish is in poor condition, or unsuitable for this new situation, you

may have to apply a new one. If the wood or metalwork is at all ornate, try to avoid stripping the piece – it will be a difficult task.

A mantel will probably last longer if you screw it to the wall. Then the bed can still be moved for cleaning but the mantel will not get pulled around. Another advantage of fixing it permanently or semi-permanently to a wall is the possibility of fitting it with lights. Tasteful lamps, in character with the style of the headboard, would add greatly to its charm and usefulness.

Coal scuttles
Among the more plentiful items available from yesteryear are metal coal scuttles, some of them made of very good quality materials. The better looking ones were intended to stand in living rooms, and are consequently worth having for their appearance alone, whether or not you put them to work. In many cases, there may be opportunities to give them back their old job, although you might prefer to clean yours out thoroughly, polish and lacquer it, and use it as a magazine rack.

Wooden scuttles are rarer, so much so that younger people could pass them by, not recognizing them for what they are. Imagine a box, upright at the back and with a flat floor sloping up a little at the front edge, to stop the coal from falling out. The front edges

of the side pieces sloped backwards quite steeply, parallel with the lid. A robust, often fussy handle sat on the lid. Another simpler handle was usually provided at the bottom edge of the lid. Most wooden scuttles were made from quite decent hardwood, and lined to some extent with steel or brass sheeting. Since they stood up to 450mm (18 inches) high, they were not the kind of things to lift up whenever you wanted to stoke the fire. A small shovel went with them for that chore.

Getting the inside of a wooden scuttle clean would not be half so feasible as scouring out a metal one. Uses to which you could reasonably put it would have to be very practical and unglamorous in character: make it into a shoe-cleaning unit, for example, and you might not even have to refinish it.

Tiffin table tops
The folding wooden underframe of a Tiffin table is more ingenious than robust, but nothing short of a furnace is likely to affect the thick, heavy-gauge brass top. These are about 600mm (about 24 inches) in diameter, and are flanged rather like a deep dinner-plate. Despite their Egyptian and oriental designs they were made primarily in England. When brightly polished they have a rich golden gleam that makes them highly effective

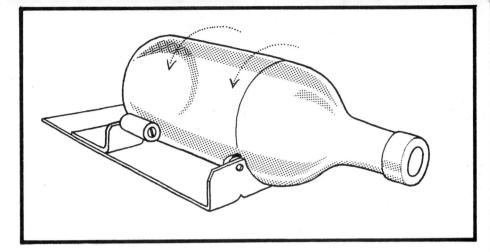

Opposite: A barrel with a stylized flower design adds a light touch to a shady corner of the garden.

as wall plaques. Drill them through the centre and plug them to the wall with a single, 75mm (3 inch) brass screw.

Alternatively, you could mount it on a stand and use it simply to screen a little-used fireplace.

Washstand jugs

Porcelain, pretty and of generous proportions, these capacious jugs were quite common in country districts about 30 to 40 years ago. Modern plumbing has made most of them redundant, and their large capacity makes them unsuitable for everyday use as pitchers. But they are wide-necked, stable and strong, and so can be most useful as umbrella stands, or as brush-holders in the toilet, instead of the light and unsteady modern plastic ones.

Failed refrigerators

Scrap an old refrigerator and you may discard a very solid and serviceable cupboard, which possesses the virtue of airtightness. However, they should *never* be left empty, or used to hold children's playthings. Children are very tempted by old refrigerators, but because they are both airtight and impossible to open from the inside, they are very dangerous if children shut themselves in. If you are not going to make use of an old refrigerator, always break the lock or take the door off.

Perhaps the safest use for an old refrigerator would be as the long-term storage cupboard for soft fruit, such as apples or pears. When kept in a confined space, they slowly choke themselves in the carbon dioxide they give off. This gas, heavier than air, settles around them, keeping their skins from the oxygen in the air that would induce them to rot.

Most refrigerators have slatted shelves of plastic-covered wire ideal for holding rows of fruits, but supplementary racks might be needed to take full advantage of the available space. Beading supports to hold the extra shelves may be stuck to the sides with an impact adhesive.

Colander to lampshade

Old metal colanders adapt themselves well to life as lampshades. They are the right shape, they have the necessary perforations to let hot air escape, they can be attractively painted and they need very little in the way of adaptation.

If your lampholder is made of metal or is in poor condition it is advisable to replace it with a modern plastic one. Establish the diameter of the hole you need to make in the colander by

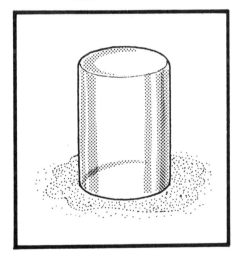

measuring the diameter of a hole in an existing lampshade.

To cut the hole in the colander, use a 'hole saw'. This consists simply of a twist drill bit with a plastic or metal collar around it which holds a specially formed piece of hacksaw blade. Once the central hole is made, the hacksaw bit acts rather like a pastry cutter. To prevent the cutter from bending the edge of the metal, support the colander on a block of wood.

Remember, when you come to decorate it use a heat-resistant paint.

New things from old bottles

Old bottles in an enormous variety of shapes and sizes are so easy to find.

Bottle cutters, available at handicraft shops or through mail-order firms, come in many forms. One type is described in the text, another (Ephrem's Olde Time Bottle Cutter) is shown above.
1. Remove the cap, then place the bottle on the cutter.
2. Lightly roll the bottle towards you, making one full turn.
3. Hold a lit candle under the line and turn the bottle in one direction slowly, then quickly.
4. Rub an ice cube over the heated line. To separate, pull lightly. Never force the pieces apart; repeat the heating process and try again.

Imagine what interesting articles could be made from bottles, if only they could be sliced across: vases, ashtrays, drinking vessels, rings, funnels, perhaps? The usual method of cutting sheet glass — scoring a line on one side, then flexing the sheet away from it on either side so that it gives way on the groove — proves to be useless on bottles.

New devices have recently been developed which solve the problem and crack bottles in predetermined places. These tools are known under various proprietary names, such as Bottle Chopper. It is a wise precaution to wear specially designed safety glasses while working

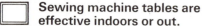
Sewing machine tables are effective indoors or out.

Strictly speaking, such bottle cutters are two tools, not one. The first consists of a jig which is anchored in the bottle neck. This jig uses the neck as a centre to guide a special glass cutter around the outside of the bottle at any pre-set height. The next step is trickier, but enjoyable. This time, you use a small weight, swung from the bottle's neck so that it will hammer precisely behind the score line. The 'hammer' dangles inside the bottle, where you induce it to swing against the side, until a crack is produced. Continue tapping around the score line until a clean break occurs all the way around. Do not try to bend the glass off by hand.

Sharp edges are smoothed with oilstones and a bit of fine oil. Finish off the edges with wet-and-dry silicon carbide paper, used wet.

Treadle sewing machine to table

In a sense, this conversion starts with a treasure — the graceful form of the cast iron under-frame. To make room for more than one pair of legs under the table, the treadle and connecting bar may have to go. Leave the wheel if you can, immobilized for safety.

Once you have removed the machine from the frame, you can lay on a new top, securing it with screws from underneath. If you would prefer to retain the original top, probably mahogany, a novel idea would be to fit a sheet of float glass accurately over it, with a photograph mounted under the section where the gap shows. There is a special printing paper for this purpose, which puts a positive transparency directly on to the glass.

OLD CLOCKS- NOT JUST A PRETTY FACE

There are so many different kinds of clock which you might encounter on the secondhand market that it is quite impossible to describe each in any detail. Here, we will deal in turn with three main types, the English fusee movement, the grandfather or long-case clock and finally, the carriage clock.

Principles of clock movements

The timing mechanism of a clock is known as *the movement*. The movement consists of a constant source of power – either a mainspring or weights – driving a number of gear wheels, which are known as *the train*. These in turn are controlled at their proper speed by the *escapement*. Escapements come in a number of designs but the most common are the anchor escapement, the lever escapement and the cylinder escapement. The complete clock is made up of the case, the movement, the pendulum and weights if fitted, the dial or clock face and the hands.

Clocks can be simple *timepieces* – by this it is meant that they do not strike or chime – or they can have a strike, or a strike and a chime. They may also be fitted with further refinements such as a repeat button – a knob which strikes the hour when pressed – and an alarm. A timepiece can be easily recognized by its single train and winding hole. A striking clock has two mainsprings, two trains and two winding holes. A chiming clock has three of each.

The gearing which transmits movement from the train to the hands is known as the *motion work*; the mechanism which permits the striking action is usually found under the dial and is known as the *strike mechanism*. Keeping these basic points in mind, let us proceed with more detailed descriptions.

The English fusee clock

Figure 1 illustrates an English fusee timepiece in a simple wood case. The back view of the clock is shown in figure 2. These clocks are very robust, have a cheerful loud tick and, when cleaned up with the case scraped and

On the table: Two striking clocks and a charming carriage clock; on the wall: two versions of the English fusee; and a splendid grandfather clock.

waxed, they make a charming addition to a wall. Fusee timepieces were made in their thousands and can still be found in shops, station waiting rooms and post offices. They are very reliable as clocks and can be regulated to a high degree of accuracy. The price of a shabby one can be extremely low, but one that has been polished up and is in working order will be five to six times as much.

Let us assume, therefore, that you have found an unloved specimen in a junk shop. What should you now look for? The first rule, which applies to all clocks, is 'do not be taken in by just a pretty case'. You should ensure that the movement can be repaired before you buy it, assuming, that is, that you want your find as a clock, and not just as an attractive ornament.

Examining the fusee clock

The clock must be examined properly. First, open the little trap-door in the side of the back, look in and see if the clock has a pendulum. If it has, unhook it (see figure 5) and take it out. If there is no pendulum, the clock may still be worth having, but it will cost at least half as much again as the clock itself to have a new one supplied and fitted.

With the pendulum out, place the clock on its back and open the glass which is usually hinged on the right side. Check the dial and hands for damage. Turn the hands forward to ensure that they are not broken or pinned loosely. Do not worry if they are not synchronized as this is easily put right.

There are specialists who can make any known part for a clock, who can make a new hand to match the one remaining and who can restore dials to their former glory. However, these things take time and money and you cannot undertake major repairs such as these by yourself. The best advice is to accept a clock with a broken glass — firms are available which will cut and bevel a new one for you — but steer clear of badly damaged hands and dials.

Checking the timing mechanism

Now to the movement itself. Having closed and secured the glass, place the clock face down on a bench. The box over the back is held in place by four dowel pegs. Remove these and lift the box off. You will now see the fusee (figure 3) from which the movement gets its name.

The fusee may at first seem complicated, but it is really a very simple mechanism. It was designed to ensure that the powerful mainspring gives a constant torque, or twist, to the train and does not fall off in power as the spring runs down. The power of the mainspring in the brass barrel is passed on to the fusee by means of a small chain or a wire line.

Once you have established that the fusee is in place, give the clock a short wind to impart a little power to the mechanism. Three or four clicks will do. If the fusee is of the chain type — it looks like a miniature bicycle chain — make sure that the chain is not broken. Chains can be repaired quite easily, but spare chains for replacement are very hard to find.

If the clock has a wire or gut line fusee, its condition is not so important, as spares are quite easy to purchase from special dealers in clock materials.

Now check the train wheels (see figure 4) for end and side shake. This should not be excessive. The train drives the *escape wheel* (figure 5) which is controlled by the *anchor*. With the pendulum off and the clock partially wound, the clock should tick fast when held in an upright position. Try this and, at the same time, observe that the hands are moving around the dial. If the train runs free, and the hands whirr around, there is something wrong with the escapement and it is advisable to look for another clock!

If the clock will not tick at all, this may be because the movement is very dirty. Move the crutch (see figure 5) from side to side and see if the escape wheel goes around. A busy tick is the best sign but, if the escape wheel turns a full 360° when you move the crutch by hand, the clock should not be too difficult to repair, although it will probably require expert attention.

The last thing to check is the pendulum. It should be straight, with a rating nut at the bottom and a suspension spring at the top. Suspension springs are often broken because the pendulum has not been unhooked in transit. However, their repair is simple and inexpensive. Similarly, a missing key for winding is no real drawback, as a dealer can easily supply one. Once your examination is complete, replace the back cover and begin to bargain with the shopkeeper.

The grandfather clock

The grandfather or long case clock is a beautiful piece of furniture, but make sure that you buy one which will fit into your house. It may seem silly to say this, but these clocks can be more than seven feet high.

Having learned how to examine a fusee timepiece, you should have no difficulty with a grandfather clock. The basic difference is that a grandfather is driven by weights, has a much longer pendulum and usually has a striking mechanism.

Face to face with the clock of your dreams, how do you look it over? Again remember not to be taken in by the case alone. Getting at the movement may seem to be something of a problem, however. The glass panels in the side of the case reveal

nothing. Do not be discouraged, it is really very simple.

Figure 6 shows how the entire hood of a grandfather clock slides forward. Open the door in the clock case and then the door covering the dial. If a catch is fitted, and often it is not, it should be on the left side of the dial door where marked. Sometimes the catch is a wooden lever operated from inside the door in the clock case. In any case try feeling for the hook with your fingers and then gently slide the hood forward until it is completely free. Be especially careful when doing this. Many an 'expert' has either dropped the hood or pulled the whole clock forward on top of himself!

The movement of a grandfather clock

Now to examine the movement. As before, start with the hands and dial, the only difference being that the movement remains in situ on the clock case. Turn the hands slowly in a clockwise direction. You should hear the strike mechanism released at the hour and possibly the half hour. Grandfather clock hands are often of an intricate design and it may be quite costly to have a broken one replaced.

If the weights of the clock are hooked on, you can test the train and escapement as for the fusee clock. If they are not, pull down on the gut lines — usually the right one as you face the clock is for the hands and the left one is for the strike. Simulate the weight in position by pulling. With a grandfather clock, you can leave the pendulum in place, swing it from side to side and watch the escape wheel revolve. If anything jams or locks, do *not* force it.

The strike mechanism is tested in the same way, but it can often be jammed. Pull on the left gut line, move the minute hand past the hour and watch the strike train revolve.

There are often parts of a grandfather clock missing. As a rough guide, pendulums, weights and bells for the strike can be obtained fairly easily at reasonable cost. However, missing gear wheels have to be redesigned and then made up and this can prove to be very expensive.

Setting up a grandfather clock

Finally, two points about setting up your clock when you get it home. Figure 7 shows three drawings which demonstrate how to secure the clock to the wall. This is very necessary, for unless the clock is held rigid, the vibration of the pendulum and the swing of the weights at the full length of their lines can cause the whole clock to sway in sympathy and bring the pendulum to a halt.

The second problem will be putting the clock in beat. Open the door of the clock case and allow the pendulum to hang still (see Figure 8). Mark

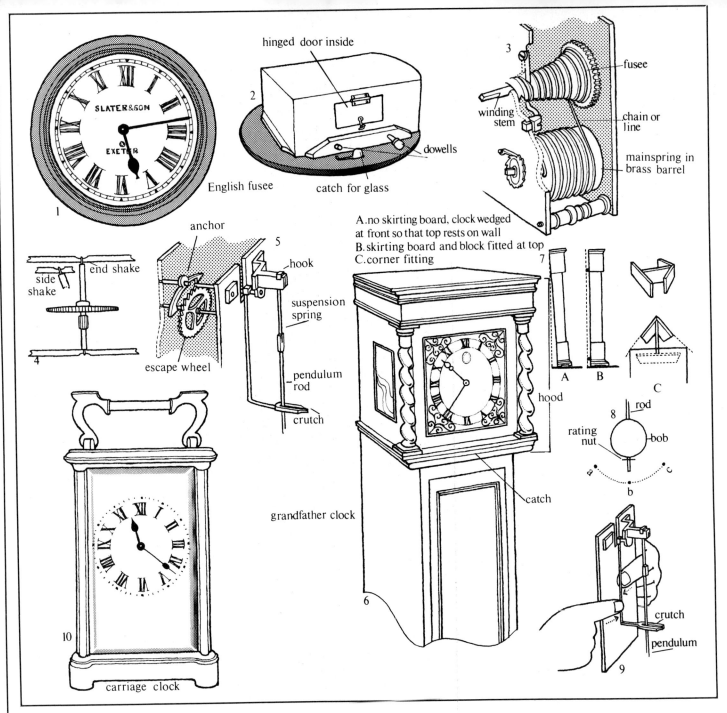

hinged door inside

2

catch for glass

dowells

English fusee

SLATER&SON

EXETER

1

3

fusee

winding stem

chain or line

mainspring in brass barrel

anchor

side shake

end shake

4

escape wheel

5

hook

suspension spring

pendulum rod

crutch

A. no skirting board, clock wedged at front so that top rests on wall
B. skirting board and block fitted at top
C. corner fitting

7

A   B

C

hood

rod

8

rating nut

bob

a   c

b

grandfather clock

catch

6

crutch

pendulum

9

10

carriage clock

where the end of the pendulum (b) hangs. Dressmakers' pins stuck in the wood at the back of the case make a good mark. Swing the pendulum to one side till it ticks and mark this position (a). Swing to the other side (c) and mark again. The arcs ab and bc must be equal if the clock is to run properly. If they are not equal, bend the crutch (figure 9) until they are. For example, if it is necessary to move the pendulum more to the left, face the clock front and gently bend the crutch to the left. Adjust in slow stages, check the swing each time, and correct until the arcs are equal.

Finally, a point about regulating the speed of the clock. For all pendulums, the higher the bob, the faster the clock will go. To make it go faster, merely wind up the rating nut to lift the bob.

Carriage clocks

In the last few years carriage clocks have become very popular, so they may be difficult to find at bargain prices. A simple timepiece is illustrated in figure 10. More complicated clocks, striking on bell or gong with repeats and alarms, can be found but are rapidly becoming very expensive.

If you do find one, wind it up, hold it by the top handle and rotate it in a horizontal plane. You should see the balance wheel through the top glass panel swing from side to side. If the movement seems sound — you cannot get your fingers at it but you can look and see whether the wheels and hands rotate — do not worry too much about the state of the case or the glass panels. The case can be electro-gilded, as was the original finish, and panels can be cut, bevelled and

replaced. You must be prepared to spend a fair amount of money on these repairs, but once done they may double the value of the clock.

Cleaning a clock

Complete instructions for cleaning a clock are quite elaborate, but these are the basics. Take the movement out of the case. Remove the hands, the dial, and the motion and striking works. Let down the mainspring by releasing the click mechanism as you control the spring carefully with the key. Dismantle the rest of the clock. Clean all the parts in benzine and polish them with metal polish before reassembling. Clean the pivot holes carefully with an orange stick. Lightly oil the mechanism, wind the clock and then, if not successful, refer to a good manual on clocks.

BONE, IVORY AND TORTOISE-SHELL

Bone is at least one substance that suffers no shortage of raw materials for replacement of broken or missing pieces. A good-sized section of leg-bone from the butcher will yield a great deal of useful, solid cutting material. However, before you put it into store for future use in repair work, you must separate the hard bone from the meat, marrow and gristle scraps that come with it.

Mending bone
Stewing it for an hour or two will soften and loosen things enough to make it possible to scrape the outside clean and remove the marrow. After this initial scraping you may need to boil it a bit more in clean water to remove all the final traces.

Almost certainly, the clean bone will be too dark in shade for some of the applications that it will be needed for, but do not bleach it too white to begin with. Soak it in a cold, dilute solution of domestic bleach until it looks reasonably uniform in shade. Remove all traces of the bleach by rinsing the bone several times in very hot water. Store it in a very dry place.

Bone can be cut with a hacksaw, whittled with a drawing knife, filed, sanded and polished. Remember it has a 'grain' so you should cut repair inserts to match in properly. Quick-setting epoxy adhesives are the most practical to use for bone repairs.

Yellow ivory
The dividing line between what some regard as deep cream and others as yellow can be a hazy one. This, of course, makes it difficult to tell if ivory has discoloured from simple aging or from staining. The safest criterion is probably the distribution of the dis-coloration. Aging-yellow will be pretty even all over, while stains will be patchy and localized.

If the item is stained to a totally unacceptable degree, bleach it very gingerly with a dilute domestic bleach. Ivory is a natural material with grain and a tendency to fine cracking, which wetting might well precipitate.

Real tortoiseshell
Like ivory, tortoiseshell was originally grown by a living creature for its own protection. Do not let sunlight play on tortoiseshell if it is in good condition because even mild heat can dry it out

and the light can bleach it. If it is a little deteriorated, try wiping it over with any natural clear oil.

Should you fail to revive the surface by this means, rub the top layer with fine-grit paper (wet-and-dry or Lubrisil) until you get to sound tissue. Polishing gently with wax to finish is all you dare do on a fragile structure. Heavier ones can be buffed with a power drill, fitted with one of the small fabric dollies. Use the polishing compound supplied in the kit which comes with the dolly.

If you can, mount the drill and polishing wheel on a bench cradle and hold the article against it with both hands. Let the motor do the work and

□ **Above: Horn beakers; an ivory-backed dressing table set; tortoiseshell napkin rings; a bone-handled carving set.**

do not press hard. Keep the wheel moving over the surface of the tortoiseshell, to avoid over-heating it.

Knife handle repairs
Traditionally, these were fixed on by melting a bituminous filler into the handle socket and setting the pointed end of the blade into it. The fixing was very strong, but even so hot water loosens many good joints. To mend, drill out the old filler if you can, and replace it with car-body resin filler.

NEW LAMPS FOR OLD

Many unusual containers or cast-off items, such as old coffee-grinders or large, globular glass bottles, can be made into attractive lamps. Several basic techniques can be learned which will then apply to almost any lamp you will make.

Bulb holders
Most lamps can be made with one of two basic types of bulb holder. One is for fitting into bottle-necks and has a long, tapering 'cork'; the other is for screw-fixing to solid bases and has a hollow plinth with some thin segments moulded into the sides. These can be nicked out cleanly if you want to bring the flex out sideways.

If your chosen base is a bottle or some other hollow and not-too-heavy vessel, it is safest to use a bulb holder which has the flex coming out through the cork. Then you can drill a hole through the glass and lead the flex through it. Avoid using the type of bulb holder with flex coming through the side, above the bottle's neck. The weight of the cable can easily pull over all but the heaviest base and it is also impossible to conceal properly.

Of course, it is possible to increase a bottle's weight and to some extent its stability, by filling it with sand or marbles. However, if the basic shape of the bottle does not give it a low centre of gravity to begin with it will not be possible to balance it properly.

Screw-on bulb holders are especially useful for fitting bulbs to solid, flat-topped lamp stands. They can be mounted over a small hole so that the wire does not need to show; many have built-in switching mechanisms — a good feature to have in any lamp.

Drilling through block bases
The sheer mass and weight of solid-block bases made from lumps of stone, slate or similarly dense material, is sufficient to counteract an accidental pull on a cable. Nevertheless they would have to be extremely heavy to be regarded as totally safe in this respect.

Drilling a hole right through the block may seem a daunting prospect, and cannot be done at all without a power drill. It will need a tungsten-carbide tipped drill bit of a large enough diameter to make a hole the cable can comfortably fit through. The bit should also be long enough to bore through the whole block from top to bottom in a single pass: do not try to reverse and drill half the hole from the opposite direction.

Soft materials such as slate can sometimes be more difficult to drill through than harder ones, most of which can be penetrated by using an impact attachment. This is a simple device which makes the drill-bit deliver short, sharp, hammer blows as it rotates. Pulverizing action like this helps to get through concrete or other intractable materials, which would otherwise blunt or overheat the tip before any inroad has been made. Not all masonry bits will stand up to impact drilling, but getting one that will is mainly a matter of asking the dealer before you buy. Impact-proof bits will usually work equally well on purely rotary applications.

Adequate support for the block while you are drilling is very important for both effectiveness and safety. This is especially true if you try to drill diagonally to bring the flex out from the side of the block, as near to the bottom as possible. If you have qualms about your ability to achieve this, drill vertically down and straight through instead. To take the cable out, you will then have to file or chisel a shallow channel under the base.

Impact drilling should present no clogging or binding problems, but you may encounter them when going through soft materials. In general, these do not respond to the impact method and should be bored with a normal, rotary bit. Chips and dust tend to become tightly packed in the flutes of the drill, thereby clogging it up.

If you can see dust or chips appearing steadily from the hole, and the tone of the motor does not vary to any marked degree, there should be no problem. Listen for a drop in the motor-speed, and for screaming noises from the drill tip. Watch for the slightest bit of smoke, or smell of it, from the hole. The trick for the prevention of this clogging is to withdraw the rotating drill at regular intervals to clear the flutes and the hole. The stickier the material you are drilling, the more often you should do it. With practice you will learn to feel and hear when it is advisable to withdraw.

A chimney-pot lamp
Your ambitions need not be confined solely to lamps of table size. Although an object such as a chimney pot may at first seem a highly unlikely suggestion, there are one or two considerations that make it perfectly practical. Both its shape and weight would make it very steady. Being hollow, it would not present a drilling problem, only the much easier one of providing anchorage at one end for the bulb holder. Highly glazed or matt surfaces can be found with a little searching and if you do not like the natural colour, painting can work wonders in transforming it.

Of course, there is not the slightest need to block in the pot at its base as it will stand quite happily on its rim, but a flat filling or cap for the top

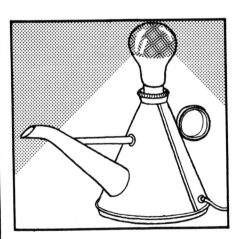
An oilcan lamp looks best with a crown-silvered bulb and does usually not require a lampshade.

Carboys, or any large globular bottles, make lovely lamps. Fit them with cork-style bulb holders.

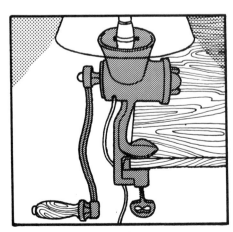
Meat mincers often make practical lamps for kitchens, as they are easy to fix on shelves.

is essential. This can be made on a once-and-for-all basis since it will never have to be removed. One way of capping the hole is to cut out two discs from hard wood, sticking them together to make a rebated 'cork'. The bottom one will have to fit inside the top as closely as possible so that resin filler or exterior grade cellulose filler can be packed around to hold it. Shape the top disc flush with the rim using a cabinet file or a medium grade abrasive paper.

An easier and probably neater method is to turn the pot upside-down on to a flat board and fill in the end to a depth of 50mm (2 inches) or so with a car-body resin filler or a proprietary cement filler. Place newspaper or plastic sheeting between the pot and the board to stop the filler from sticking. Both are quite easy to scrape off after drying, but a bit of grease on the upper surface of the plastic sheeting will avoid even that necessity. In any case, the filler will have to be sanded or filed smooth and flush with the top rim so that the bulb holder can be screwed in place. Before doing this, however, drill the chimney-pot to take the cable and paint it. Finally drill a hole in the wall of the pot near the base to lead the flex out and then fit the bulb holder and lampshade.

Solid wood bases
Whether these bases take the form of a smoothed and finished oblong or cube, or of a fat log, the difficulty lies in boring a hole down the grain. Always a troublesome operation, such drilling is rarely successful because there is never enough resistance to screw-action to give the auger a positive grip. The longer the hole and the less seasoned the wood, the more difficult it becomes.

Diagonal drilling is the shortest solution, probably starting from a point nearer the edge of the wood block to reduce the length of hole

needed. Even this expedient, however, will need quite a long drill bit, one not readily available to the home craftsman.

There are two feasible do-it-yourself methods to choose from. If drilling by hand, you can get Scotch-eyed augers, which have a special hole going across the shank to take a special 'tommy'-bar. Enormous leverage can be applied with moderate effort. Otherwise hire a heavy-duty power drill that has a slow speed and a very powerful twist; drill very intermittently, preferably in a horizontal direction with the log anchored firmly to a bench. Clear chips often and carefully.

Oilcan lamps
Old-style oilcans sometimes have novel contours which will make intriguing shapes for lamps. Most that you find will be made from tinplate, rather heavy-gauge, and the seams will be prominent, folded over and brazed. Any oil remaining inside must be washed away. Methylated spirit is probably the safest solvent to use, although caution is still needed as it is flammable.

An oilcan lamp would probably look ludicrous if fitted with a shade, but you will still need to fit a fairly large bulb holder just to accommodate one of the smaller, screw-fitting, candle-style bulbs. Try to get one with a screw-collar, for which you can drill a hole approximately the right size and fix with epoxy or resin filler. When you lead out the cable somewhere near the bottom of the can, fit a rubber 'grummet' into the hole to stop the flex being cut: electrical suppliers stock them in assorted sizes. If the outer surface is still unattractive after you have cleaned it up, use an antique metallic paint to re-finish it.

Jar-type bases
Glass measuring jars normally have quite heavy bases which make them suitable for conversion into lamps.

Above: Plain lampshades can be decorated in numerous ways to dress up an old lamp. This one has been marbled using the techniques discussed earlier.

Their tops may be too wide for cork-type holders, so it may be necessary to make wooden lids for the screw-type holders.

Large carboy-style jars are often used to contain drinks such as draught cider. Their globular shape is very attractive and these bottles are little trouble to convert.

Plastic embedding kits can also provide good lamp bases. Use large, fat moulds which are available as additions to the basic kit.

Lampshade proportion
Generally, two basic requirements must be satisfied when fitting lampshades. First choose a shade which shields the eyes of the person sitting in the lowest seat in the room. Secondly, be sure that the shade is tall enough to keep the light from dazzling a six-footer when standing up. If you satisfy these conditions, the shade proportions should be accurate. If in doubt, choose a slightly oversize shade.

For a quaint-looking lamp, use an old coffee grinder, painted or varnished for a pretty finish.

Some of the most interesting shapes for lamps can be found in odd pieces of driftwood.

An exploded view of a cork-style bulb holder with the wiring attached.

MIX AND MATCH FURNITURE ARRANGE-MENTS

Rooms with a blend of furniture styles and finishes tend to be more interesting and warmer in feeling than those which do not mix-and-match. By acquiring an eye for colours and a strong sense of proportion it is possible to mix almost anything with a reasonable amount of success.

Opposites attract

It is a general rule that every furniture shape needs a counterpoint in order to be fully appreciated. In furnishings opposites *do* sometimes attract, and very effectively too. Low lines need the occasional tall shape; severe planes can be set off by some round, squashy shapes, such as large floor-cushions.

Split-level interior

A close look at this modern, split-level room will reveal that it has been furnished with a well-chosen mixture of modern and not-so modern pieces.

On the lower level the modern, light-wood rectangular tables have been paired with several traditional bent-wood chairs. These have been rubbed down smooth with a medium-grade abrasive paper and painted cheerful colours in gloss paints. A clear polyurethane lacquer finish over the paint will give the chairs excellent protection against scuffs and scrapes.

The armchair in the foreground has been re-upholstered in a smart-looking modern stripe which both flatters its curved high back and blends it in with the clean lines of the room.

The upper-level bedroom has been given a charming touch by the addition of the miniature pet's house in the left-hand corner and the iron-based oval table with the globular glass fish bowl on top. The pet's house could be finished in any number of ways, but here it has been left in its natural wood finish and given a good polish for protection. The iron-base of the table has had all traces of rust removed (see pages 38–39) and been painted a soft cream colour.

On the right the stool has been rubbed down with abrasive paper and then painted in a gloss-finish lime green to compliment the other greens in the room. A small round cushion was made to cover a scruffy-looking seat.

The kitchen

Pine and country-look furniture of almost any period is a popular choice for older style buildings with high ceilings and large rooms. In this kitchen, the furniture has been carefully stripped down and the natural wood surface left to view. If the wood is at all dry, it is advisable to rub in a coat or two of boiled linseed oil and finish with a good wax polish.

To complete the old-fashioned look in the room, the cabinet doors at the left were cleverly finished with old ceramic tiles. These were fixed in place with a synthetic latex adhesive.

Dining room

The very comfortable, plush look of this dining room has been created in part by the use of soft fabrics – even on the walls – and by the combination of beautifully finished natural wood tables and cabinets with the more casual cane and basketweave chairs and catch-alls.

The cane chairs were in good shape and needed mainly a good clean with a rag, brush and warm soapy water. Afterwards they were painted black using a spray gun; an aerosol would work just as well.

Besides the textures, the proportions of the various pieces work very well together – tall at the back wall, oval in the centre, and long rectangular along the right-hand wall.

Glossary of Basic Terms

Alkyd Paints: Water-based paints. These are quick-drying and now are quite tough, but still not as hard-wearing as polyurethanes.

Abrasive Paper: There are any number of different grades and types of this paper – i.e. flour paper, emery paper, garnet paper. Ask your local dealer which type to use for a specific task.

Enamel: Either a vitreous composition fired over a surface to give a hard, gloss finish, or a glossy paint which forms a hard, smooth coat.

French Polish: A traditional polish made mainly of shellac dissolved in methylated spirit.

Glaze: A very thin, transparent tint of colour applied directly to wood or over a clear finish lacquer. The term is used more generally to mean any substance which will give a clear or translucent shiny finish to a surface.

Japanning: To give a high gloss to a surface. The term originates from the Japanese technique of applying layers of lacquer (usually black) to build up a shiny finish.

Polyurethane: Any of a specific group of chemical compounds (polymers) used in various resins, paints and lacquer finishes. They give an extremely tough, hardwearing finish.

Scumble: Generally speaking, a very thin coat of opaque colour. In imitation wood graining, a thin glaze which is applied in two layers – a dark one and a light one which are combed or blended together.

Spackle: A very fine filler for small holes or dents in wood surfaces. Available in a proprietary mix. Decorators often make their own from finely ground plaster of Paris, linseed oil and a tint.

Thixotropic: A technical term used by many paint manufacturers to indicate that a paint is non-drip.

Varnish: A term used to denote a clear protective finish. There are many different types – some based on wood resins, others on synthetic cellulose constituents and others on shellac and a volatile spirit mixture. Modern varnishes are usually made of clear plastic lacquers.

Wood Stain: Either a chemical mix or a proprietary mix which alters the colour of wood. There are natural tints and brilliant colours.

We should like to thank the following firms for their help in lending accessories for photography:

Berger Paints
Freshwater Road, Dagenham, Essex

Christopher Wray's Lighting Emporium
King's Road, London SW3

Dan Klein
10 Canonbury Place, London SW3

Designer's Guild
King's Road, London SW3

Dunlop
Ryder Street, London SW1

Furniglas
136 Great North Road, Hatfield

Furniture Cave
King's Road, London SW3

Liden Whitewood Limited
227 Lea Bridge Road, London E10

Richard Morris
Wandsworth Bridge Road, London SW6

RTS Displays
Flood Street, London SW3

Sanderson Wallpapers and Paints
Berners Street, London W1

Selfridges Limited
Oxford Street, London W1

Strike One
1a Camden Walk, London N1

T. F. Buckle
King's Road, London SW3

T & S Lemkow
9 Pierrepoint Arcade, London N1

Photographs by
Armstrong Cork Company: pages 39, 64
Steve Bicknell: pages 5, 11, 13, 18, 19, 21, 23, 28, 34, 37, 39, 40, 41, 47, 50, 56, 59
Michael Boys: page 5
Camera Press: pages 10, 17, 24, 25, 27, 39, 42, 54, 55, 62, 63
Heidede Carstensen: pages 15, 46, 54
Nelson Hargreaves: page 31
Graham Henderson/Young Colour Magazine: pages 17, 51
John Ledger: page 52
Chris Lewis: pages 43, 45, 48-49
John Sullivan: page 61
Liz Whiting/Lavinia Press: pages 1, 15
Zefa: page 17

Text David Fisher
Illustrations Kate Simunek
Picture Stylist
    and Consultant Heather Standring
Assistant Editor Jeanne Sullivan
Art Editor Andrzej Bielicki
Assistant Art Editor Judith Robertson

Metric equivalents given within the text are approximate only, and are intended as a guide to sizes and measurements.